Aleta

The Slow Good-Bye

Melecio A. Valdez

iUniverse, Inc.
Bloomington

Aleta
The Slow Good-Bye

iUniverse books may be ordered through booksellers or by contacting:

iUniverse
1663 Liberty Drive
Bloomington, IN 47403
www.iuniverse.com
1-800-Authors (1-800-288-4677)

Because of the dynamic nature of the Internet, any web addresses or links contained in this book may have changed since publication and may no longer be valid. The views expressed in this work are solely those of the author and do not necessarily reflect the views of the publisher, and the publisher hereby disclaims any responsibility for them.

Any people depicted in stock imagery provided by Thinkstock are models, and such images are being used for illustrative purposes only.

Certain stock imagery © Thinkstock.

ISBN: 978-1-4620-2237-3 (sc)
ISBN: 978-1-4620-2238-0 (hc)
ISBN: 978-1-4620-2239-7 (e)

Library of Congress Control Number: 2011908509

Printed in the United States of America

iUniverse rev. date: 06/15/2011

This book is dedicated to my wife, Aleta Corre Valdez, and my children, Amihan Valdez Barker (daughter), Richard Barker II (son-in-law), Magdiwang Ruel Valdez (son), and Rebecca Davis Valdez (daughter-in-law), and my grandchildren, Ashtin Barker and Richard Barker III (Tre).

Acknowledgments

Special thanks to all friends and relatives who helped me to put together this book into reality: Dr. and Mrs. Carlito Asperas, Mrs. Rebecca Davis-Valdez, designer Diwang Valdez, Reverend Amihan Valdez-Barker, and Richard Barker II and Carlmax Frie Valdez for their technological assistance.

Contents

Chapter 1

Going Home

On February 20, 2008, I was at JCPenny looking at some bathroom rugs for sale when suddenly I got a call from Athens Adult Day Care Center. Aleta (who preferred to be called Leth) was on her way to the emergency room of Athens Regional Medical Center. She had fallen from what they thought was a seizure, and her head hit the edge of the bathroom door, which caused a lot of bleeding.

She was just coming in when I got to the emergency room. The doctors and medical staff did all the standard procedures to take care of her. Her attending doctor decided to confine her for further study to examine what caused her to fall. Neurologist Dr. Novy ruled out a seizure. They took X-rays but found out nothing except that her dementia, Alzheimer's, was progressing. Leth, who used to walk, talk, and move around, suddenly seemed to give up. I tried to help her sit and stand. I guessed she was trying but her mind could not tell her body what to do.

After nine days in the hospital, Dr. Bullecer, her family doctor and a Filipino, told me to take her to a nursing home for rehabilitation, as there they might be able to help her sit, stand, and walk again. Ed and Carla, the physical therapists, did all they could to help her back on her feet but found it hopeless. She was not responding to any of their commands. After twenty days in rehabilitation, I found no development except for her continuous loss of speech and mobility.

When we decided to buy land and build a house by the beach in Baler, Aurora, we dreamed about going to the Philippines to retire. The original plan was to leave after our son's planned wedding on October 4,

2008. We did not expect to leave until these circumstances occurred. I called my brother-in-law, who had been managing the building of our house. He indicated that the house was done except for a few finishing touches.

My family had a meeting to discuss what was best for Leth and the whole family. The meeting was so emotional and was not easy for any of us. Now that twenty days of rehabilitation were over, the family had to decide whether we would let her stay in a nursing home or provide at-home care. Leth needed twenty-four-hour care, but at-home care was limited and I could not take care of her due to my own poor health condition. Dr. Bullecer advised against my taking care of her due to my heart problem.

The nursing home seemed to be the only alternative, but Leth had made me promise that I would never take her to a nursing home. We discussed all the pros and cons of the issue. I asked doctors and some other medical experts for their opinions. Since Alzheimer's has no cure, all we needed to do was give the best quality care we could provide, and going to the Philippines seemed to be the best alternative. The money we would have used for a nursing home in the United States could go further in the Philippines.

What about the kids and grandkids? A large number of relatives on both sides of our family were in the United States. I listened and prayed fervently for a good decision. I made up my mind. My priority would be for the quality of Leth's care—to be with her and stay with her for the rest of our lives. Our kids understood my decision and gave me their full blessing. Diwang, our son, said, "I would rather see you with Mom than go every day to a nursing home at a certain time." Amy and Rich, our daughter and son-in-law, seemed to see the total picture, that Leth would no longer recognize them soon. It was a sad situation, but it was the reality we all needed to face.

Time passed quickly, and I knew that she would not recognize us any longer. What mattered to me was that I would love her, take care of her, and give her the best quality care I could provide. The cost of a nursing home in the United States was more than enough for me to provide her quality personalized care in the Philippines. I had assessed that I could afford to give her twenty-four-hour operation care from professional and experienced caregivers. Three of Leth's siblings seemed to disagree with our plans. One even suggested that I should take her to California where they live, and rent an apartment there, and she and her kids would take care of her. She said she wanted to serve her sister to compensate for what Leth did for them when they were growing up. Leth had worked hard to raise them. She was the eldest in the family.

Elaine, the third eldest in the family, and the youngest brother, Emeritus, came to visit her. Elaine spent time with her in the rehabilitation center, feeding her, talking to her, and massaging her. She and I had a long visit prior to her going home to Canada. I explained to her how I had made the decision to go back to the Philippines. She seemed to understand. I told her that my priority was the quality of her sister's care, our relationship, and being together in the last period of her lifetime. I wanted to spend my time with her and give her the best care I could give.

I thought I made myself clear. My priority was my wife and not the children, nor the grandkids, nor the siblings. My family supported and understood my position. The plan was finalized, and we contacted her relatives in the Philippines. We were supposed to leave by April 2008. We contacted the air ambulance so that they could provide us with a quote of expenses. Including a nurse for the round-trip travel would cost around $25,000 (this was not even in an air ambulance, but rather on a commercial flight).

Leth's doctor said that all I needed for travel was someone who could help me carry her in case of incontinence or other unexpected incidents. Leth had a very strong heart. She didn't need any respiratory assistance. Amy called several airlines to find out the cost for my son-in-law's and my travel without a nurse. It would cost me only $12,500. It was inexpensive enough, so I felt somewhat relieved due to the tight situation I was in.

Ed, the occupational therapist, and Dr. Brown of the Grandview Nursing Home were instrumental in helping us acquire a customized wheelchair and a hydraulic manual lift, both necessary for our travel and future use once we got to the country. We packed all necessary equipment for our air travel, and all the excess was put in *balikbayan* boxes—a term used for standardized freight boxes sent to the Philippines, for cargo shipping.

The day of travel finally came. On April 23, 2008, we left Athens at around 2:00 AM and arrived at least two hours before the actual flight at Hartsfield-Jackson Atlanta International Airport. Amy was driving my Cadillac DeVille with Leth and me while Rich was driving Diwang's pickup loaded with the wheelchair, the lift, and eight boxes. On my way I was praying for a safe journey. I knew that my decision was indeed a good one for Leth. I had a feeling of inner confidence, because friends and members of our church had been praying for us.

We reached the airport. My son and his fiancée, Becca Davis, arrived shortly. The transition of checking in was not that bad. The staff from the continental airline was very helpful. Our flight—which went from Atlanta, Georgia, to Houston, Texas, then to Honolulu, Hawaii, then to Guam, and finally to Manila, Philippines—was approximately twenty-six hours. From Texas to Hawaii, Leth slept well, as we were sitting in the front row of first class. Since no one was sitting close to us, the commander was kind enough to move Rich to the first-class cabin too because he had been so helpful to me as well as to them.

When I was in the bathroom, someone suddenly knocked at the door. I gave a replied knock to signify it was occupied. But the second and third knock sounded urgent, so I had to hurry. When I got out, Richard was holding her upright because she was wet and her diaper had leaked. Two of the stewardesses helpfully raised the blanket to cover her as we changed her diaper. When we reached Honolulu, she was wet again and the diaper didn't seem big enough to hold the urine. I started to worry because I only prepared three diapers and three pairs of pants in our carry-on bag, one for every stopover. The worst thing was that I forgot to put the wet ones in one carry-on bag when Amy and I changed her prior to our departure in Athens, Georgia.

We had not reached Guam yet, and she was wet again. I tried to limit her liquid intake, but even so it did not work as I had planned. I had to dig into some of our suitcases. One of the carry-on bags had an unopened box of diapers. I did not realize I had put it in there as an emergency aid in case we had an unexpected delay or stopover. It worked very well when we arrived in Guam. We changed her and made her comfortable. The trip from Guam to Manila was just four hours, but then she was wet again.

We arrived in Manila on time, but we were the last ones to get out because of some assistance that the airline provided for handicapped passengers. Furthermore, we had to claim the broken left handrail of the new wheelchair we brought with us, which caused more of a delay.

We got outside of the Manila Ninoy Aquino International Airport. The people I was expecting to come and get us were not around, so I had to get out from the gate and hunt for them. Finally, I found my brother-in-law and asked him to drive the vehicle near the airport arrivals to pick up our luggage. The nurse and her staff took care of Leth while the rest were loading the other vehicle. We went to Bulacan for a two-hour rest before we proceeded to our final destination of Baler, Aurora. The travel took between six and eight hours, depending on the traffic.

We reached Cabanatuan City at dawn. We bought some *pandesal* (breakfast bread) and had some coffee. We reached the mountain as the sun began to rise. It took us four hours traveling a winding road. Some parts of the road were cemented, but the large portion was still a rocky, rough winding road. Leth was wet again, and after an hour or two she started vomiting, perhaps due to the bumpy road. We had to stop and reposition Leth to clean her. Once again we proceeded slowly until we reached our new home, Ashtintin Beach House, at Barangay Buhangin, Baler, Aurora, Philippines.

It was our first time seeing the house they (my brother-in-law) built for us. I was very pleased by what his crew built. It was handicap accessible, as I had requested. My son-in-law was also impressed. He said, "It's awesome." The frontal landscape before the beach was done well, while at the back were three fishponds full of tilapia, mudfish, and other species. Behind the house was also a big hole for a proposed swimming pool. It was unbelievable how far our dollar could go in the country.

The house was two stories but could be three stories since the attic could be converted into a nice spacious activity room. Another nice thing was that the attic provided a panoramic view of the beach and Baler Bay. The cool breeze from the ocean seemed nonstop. I told Leth, "Honey, this is our new home." We dreamed to build our vacation or retirement home here, we bought this place, and now we were here. But I was not sure whether she could appreciate it or if it mattered to her at all. What I got from her was a blank stare; perhaps it was confusion and her wondering where in the world I took her. I wished she could talk back to me. She seemed to try, but I could not understand what she was trying to communicate. Her vocabulary was limited now to "yes" and "no," or sometimes she would raise her hands to show approval or disapproval. Or she might cry, smile, scream, or make noises just to let us know that she could still communicate in her own ways.

In my solitude I could not help but pray, sob, and cry. She asked me many times, when she could still talk, "Why is this happening to me, Mel? Why is this happening to us?" I would have liked to give her a theological word of comfort, but I found no answer except to remain silent, cry with her, and say the words: "I don't know." Both of us were clergy. Both of us loved the Lord. Did we have the right to question God? Or did we just need to accept her condition as it was and move within our affliction?

Two laypeople came to visit us from the Maria Aurora United Methodist Church (UMC). One of them could not help but ask me, "With all these things going on with you and your wife, how does your faith hold you?" The question came as a surprise, but I had to give them an answer not just as an individual believer but also as a clergy. After all, I was still a United Methodist clergy.

I said, "I am hurt, and I am still hurting. Do I blame God? I don't think so. Look around us. Young and old, some of us get sick, some of us die at a young age, and others die in old age. Sickness exists because of human failures. Some illnesses are caused by natural disasters, some because of unknown phenomena that we cannot understand. Being human means that we are subject to all of these circumstances and it has nothing to do with blaming God. Who are we to blame God? We must be grateful instead for the blessing of health and life. God gave us the opportunity to enjoy this life, even in the short period of time, and the opportunity to share this life with those whom we love and those who love us."

Blaming God in all these circumstances was being narrow-minded, as far as I was concerned. I was grateful indeed for all the blessings God bestowed upon me, especially my beautiful family and my wife. I would indeed be forever grateful to Him. Had my faith been weakened by these ailments? I didn't think so. If I didn't have a strong theological understanding of my God, it might have weakened my faith. Since I believed I had known God well enough, my faith in Him remained stronger as I faced challenges that tested my faith. I prayed and hoped that I could remain faithful and loyal as Christ's disciple until the time God would be ready to meet me.

Chapter 2

The Beginning

It was the day of martial law under Ferdinand Marcos's regime. All schools were closed. Uprising among students was temporarily suppressed. I went to Manila that week from Cabanatuan City. It was a good time to go since no one was at school. That was also the time when I got an invitation to go to a seminary in the United States, and I was in the process of working for my necessary papers at the US Embassy. I stayed in the house of a close friend who was once my senior pastor at Cabanatuan City Temple United Methodist Church. Reverend Marcelino Casuco was then the pastor of Knox Memorial Church in Manila under the Ilocano congregation. He and his wife were a lovely couple and had a good reputation as being matchmakers for young single pastors.

Pastor Casuco said that he knew a young lady, a schoolteacher, whom he wanted me to meet. I got so excited by the idea, and I waited near the gate of the church with anticipation. Miss Aleta Corre came to see Reverend C. T. Garcia, and on her way out she greeted Reverend Casuco, who introduced her to me. Reverend Casuco made an arrangement to invite her and her friend Nelly to have lunch with us the following day. Reverend Casuco was thinking of Nelly for me, but before I saw her, there seemed to be some attraction and chemistry developing between me and Aleta.

I finally met Nelly at lunchtime. I knew there and then that I was more attracted to Aleta than her friend Nelly. Aleta was so energetic, vibrant, always smiling, helpful, and beautiful. She loved the church so much and was very prayerful. I knew then in my heart that this was the woman I wanted to spend my entire life with.

After I met her, I would go to where she was teaching. At first she was surprised to see me waiting for her at the school gate after the long day of teaching grade school. "What are you doing here?" she would ask. And I always said, "I just wanted to see you and be with you." I could tell from her smiles that she liked me too.

She started to tell me what she did after school. She went to the elite subdivisions to tutor some kids for extra money to help her poor family. She and her dad, who was a bus driver, seemed to be the greatest providers for their family's daily needs. On Sundays she would take all her brothers and sisters to church, mothering them. Despite all these trips, she never missed her volunteer work at the church, teaching Sunday school, Bible classes, etc. She made more money than I did as a pastor. I said to myself, "If this lady will love me, I have it made."

Since I didn't know much about the city, she took me around Manila. She taught me how to ride in a passenger jeep. She showed me the nicest places to see. She even assisted me whenever she could to help me process my papers. As days went by, she and I felt more and more comfortable with each other, and I felt like I needed to confront her about my intentions. I needed to find out if this relationship was going to be more than friendship. I wanted her to be my life partner.

At the Luneta park, a hangout known for young lovers, while looking at Manila Bay, I told her my intention. I knew that she also had two or three admirers whom her parents and siblings liked. I knew then that I had to give her ample time to think it through to honor the time a traditional Filipina woman must take in order to preserve her dignity. (Traditionally, a Filipina woman is not allowed to show eagerness or enthusiasm towards the opposite gender. She should not respond quickly, for it would be the characteristics of an undignified woman.) However, I made it clear that I wanted to know her response the following day. She looked at me and said, "You are too fast!"

I said, "I am sorry. I feel like we have a mutual desire for each other, but I am not really sure. Now that you know my sacred intention, I would like to hear it from you. I feel tormented not knowing your desire for me. I promise that when you say yes, I will love you forever. If you say no, I promise I will never bother to ask and see you again."

Both of us separated, saying nothing to each other but agreeing to meet at the Manila Aquarium.

That night, I could not sleep thinking about what she would say. If she said no, what would I do? I loved this woman. I started to rationalize and thought of some other prospective ladies who would like me. I knew it was silly and childish, but it was a way to cover up my insecurity. Since I felt strongly that I really loved this woman, I prayed that God would make a way to make this courtship easier.

She was already waiting for me when I got to the aquarium park. I was nervous, but she gave me a smile. She took me around the aquarium park and eventually to the garden. I could hardly wait, so I cornered her and said, "I want to know the answer."

She looked at my eyes, and then I saw her tears flowing. I knew then her answer. We embraced each other and she said, "Yes, I love you and want you, too, in my life."

We kissed each other with intensity, full of love and respect. There was so much joy between us. I gave her the famous quotation from Ruth 1:16–17:

> Don't ask me to leave you! Let me go with you. Wherever you go, I will go; wherever you live, I will live. Your people will be my people, and your God will be my God. Wherever you die, I will die, and that is where I will be buried. May the Lord's worst punishment come upon me if I let anything but death separate me from you.

We went to different places, holding each other tight, kissing, holding hands, walking, talking, and playing. One night when the Casucos were out of town, I took her to my room. I told her I wanted to see her naked. She was surprised. She thought I was kidding. She looked at me and then she knew I was serious. At first she resisted the idea. She was so tense and nervous, but I smiled and whispered to her, "I'd like to see what I am going to get. Please!" I slowly undressed her while she closed her eyes, as if she was so embarrassed. I said, "I have not seen any woman naked except in pictures or in magazines." As she exposed her own body to me, I said, "You are really beautiful." Her eyes remained closed until I gave her back her clothes and helped her get dressed. "Now I know what I am going to get," I said. She pinched me.

I told her that all my papers needed for schooling had been approved. All documents were in place except one thing—I was sick. I was coughing up phlegm excessively, which caused some embarrassment. Prior to that, I had consulted a recommended physician who was supposed to be an expert on tuberculosis. He told me that there was a spot found on my lung. I religiously followed everything he advised me to do for almost three months, but to no avail. My health condition remained the same. I was so worried that I asked to be confined at Mary Johnston Hospital and sought another doctor's opinion. After an intensive examination, the doctor ruled out everything other than excessive coughing. He gave me some medications that quickly eased my case. The doctor handed me the negative X-ray results and told me that I was now free to go to the United States. I was so mad at the first doctor who diagnosed me with tuberculosis because he had taken advantage of me.

After receiving a clean bill of health and approval to go to the United States, I was determined to get married prior to my leaving the country. I asked my parents about my intention and invoked their blessing. I told Leth to do the same. We had to coordinate the schedule of Aleta's parents with that of my parents so they could come from the Quezon province to Manila, an 8-hour journey. Leth and her parents waited patiently that fateful night. I was at Reverend Casuco's parsonage anxiously waiting for them. I had to take them to Leth's residence in Matimtiman, Tondo, Manila. It was almost eleven o'clock in the evening but they had not yet arrived. I was so upset. Leth was already crying, thinking I had changed my mind. It was 11:30 PM when they arrived. They had been delayed due to transportation and road problems via Maria Aurora to Manila.

My father was so hesitant to go because it was late, but I insisted that they wait for him. Leth, who was patiently waiting for us, let out a big sigh when she saw us coming. Although her parents had already been in bed, they ushered us in. Our parents met each other while Leth and I prayed that things would go smoothly. The meeting was brief. Her dad was more receptive than her mom. They were very cordial and asked us to stay to eat, but my dad cordially responded that it was already too late and understood that Leth's dad had to work early in the morning as a bus driver. They told us that we needed to plan for a wedding quickly so that I could have at least a few days with her before leaving Manila, Philippines, to Kansas City, Missouri.

The wedding was scheduled for the first of February, and my departure for the United States was scheduled for February 19, 1971. Everything went fast. We met in November 1970, and within three months we were married. As we planned for our marriage, we grew closer. We visited some of her relatives, and my relatives, because there would be no time following the wedding. We visited my cousin, Reverend Emmanuel Tabelisma, who I called Kuya Eming. He was then planning to get married prior to our wedding. Kuya Eming gave us his room, where we could rest while he was doing his pastoral visitation. His parsonage was big enough and had rooms that had private, secluded rooms. Both of us were burning with such passion that she decided she was ready to go all the way. Well, we were about to get married anyway, so I decided to let our passion overwhelm us. Suddenly, I realized it was wrong and quickly stood up and said, "Let us save this special moment for after our wedding."

She too quickly stood up, got dressed, and said, "Yes, let us make our wedding a very special one."

We took a long nap. When we woke up, Kuya Eming was already in the house and smiling at us. He whispered to me, "Did you do it, Mel?"

I said, "Nope!" and just smiled.

I was busy getting ready to go to the United States while Leth was busy arranging all the necessities for the wedding. She had so many special friends who helped her and donated things she needed. She gave me the money for the wedding expenses, which included the reception at Goldilocks Restaurant. Three prominent Manila clergies performed the wedding: the reverends Garcia, Casuco, and Sarmiento. All these clergies were our godparents, so it was free of charge to use Knox

Memorial United Methodist Church. It turned out to be a semi-grand wedding with minimal expenses.

Baguio City, the country's tourist spot, was Leth's first choice for our honeymoon. Fortunately, the Sarmientos were heading in the same direction, so it saved us again from paying bus fare. Another good thing was that the Sarmientos knew cottages for American missionaries that were so inexpensive, unlike some hotels. Leth said, "The Lord has been really good to us. God always provides what we need." I just smiled and pondered all the blessings that God was providing us.

It had rained on our wedding day, and when we arrived in Baguio City, it was raining too. She told me, "Any first big event I do in my life, it rains." I did not believe such things, but she had always seemed right since I met her. As we got closer to our destination, my passion and desire for her were getting stronger and I could hardly wait. Then suddenly she whispered, "I just got my monthly period." I didn't understand first what that meant. So she had to explain.

I said, "I don't care. I waited for this for so long. Let us do it and make it right."

After checking in, we got the key to our room. I quickly undressed. She was so shy that I had to help her as we headed for the shower. It was the first time for both of us, and we were not quite sure what to do. Our first sexual encounter was not so pleasurable. She was in pain, and there was so much blood. I felt so disappointed. I thought I had failed her, but she was so passionate and understanding. So we did it again a second time, a third, and more and more. It was only then that she and I started enjoying our sexual play. We learned to show each other what was pleasurable and what was not.

From Baguio City, we went to my hometown, San Jose, Maria Aurora, Quezon. We had to butcher two big pigs. Leth wondered why we needed two big pigs if it was just for the family. I said, "For any wedding celebration here in town, the whole town comes, even without an invitation." Indeed, I was right. I saw so many faces that came that I didn't know. But they were there to enjoy the food and the festivity.

I scolded one of my brothers, Juanito, the clown of the family, about his old clothes, which were improper for the occasion. My wife overhead him respond, "I would have new clothes if you did not get married." Maybe he was jealous, maybe he was just joking, like he always does, but I didn't realize that Leth was hurt by that comment. She thought she had not been accepted by the family. However, the joyous celebration overcame her fear of non-acceptance.

In a few more days I was about to fly to the United States. Leth took me to Cavite and other places around Manila to meet her relatives. We didn't have much money so I had to depend on her income for our daily expenses. I only had eleven dollars in my pocket, which I was trying to save for my trip to the United States. At her family's home, I was a little bit uncomfortable because I knew that my wife was one of the breadwinners. Now she was married. This meant that her income would be removed from their budget. I also sensed some resistance from her mom about the marriage. We agreed that, while I was gone, she would work to support her family and I would try to send money whenever I could. I also asked my dad to visit my wife often and bring some of our agricultural products to help her and her family. Leth said she was not expecting much from me since I was going to school.

Time flew by. It was February 19, 1971, the day I had to fly to the United States. There was lots of hugging and crying the night prior to the flight date. At the airport, friends and relatives came to see me leave. Leth did not cry then, and we both hugged as I departed. It was my first time entering an airport. There were so many military personnel because of martial law. Every person who entered the flight gates was carefully scrutinized. Airport immigration officers had lists of people who were considered anti-government or what was known as the "black list." There were a few of us who were separated for questions. I started perspiring, wondering what would happen.

A military man asked me why my name was on the black list. I looked him in his eyes and said, "I don't know, sir. I am not a violent man and I never hurt anybody. I am just an ordinary local pastor trying to preach the gospel." After talking to the commander in charge, he let me go. That was a big relief. I proceeded to the airline gate as fast as I could without looking back. I knew my name was probably on the black list because I was active during my college years as leader of the resistance of the Marcos regime. It was good the interviewer was not that pushy and did not ask too many questions. Perhaps he didn't know what to ask, or maybe it was another intervention by God in my favor. However, that event scared me a lot.

Finally, I was in the airplane. I was overwhelmed by the new experience. This was the first flight of my life. As the plane ascended, I felt so thrilled, anticipating a new world for me to see. On the airplane, I was asked if I needed coffee. I thought it could be expensive to have coffee on the plane, so I politely said no. Then it was time for lunch. There were two menus from which to choose. Knowing I had only eleven dollars in my pocket, I politely said to the flight attendant, "No, ma'am, I am not hungry." I looked at everybody who was eating, and no one was paying for their food. So I asked the person close to me how much the lunch cost. Only then I found out that it was included when I paid my flight ticket. Since I was so embarrassed to ask for food, I waited for the second round and finally got a snack and then, after a while, a good meal.

I wished I was told what to expect as a first-time rider of an airplane, but it was too late to think about it. I learned a lesson the hard way. At breakfast time, the flight attendant came again and asked me if I wanted coffee. I said, "Yes!"

"You want black?"

I thought that was a ridiculous question. I knew that all coffee was black. So I said, "Of course, I want black." So she gave me a plain coffee without sugar or cream. Again, I found out that coffee for the Anglos was not served automatically with cream and/or sugar, unlike in the Philippines. These little things started to expose me slowly to a new culture.

I reached Honolulu, Hawaii. It was the port of entry to the United States. I was glad someone knew me and called me quickly. He saw me following a group of people to the baggage claim, which was near the exit of the airport. The man graciously said, "I thought you were going to Kansas City. This is only Hawaii. You still have a long way to go." Then, I hung out with that man and asked him questions about the United States.

Chapter 3

The Schooling

My welcoming committee included Dr. D. Houts, the seminary registrar of Saint Paul School of Theology in Kansas City, Missouri, and Carol Moe, a former Filipino missionary, along with two seminary students, who came to meet me at the airport. They were my hosts and helped orient me to my new surroundings. February 1971 was a very cold month, and there was snow on the ground. I looked at my new surroundings; and thought, this doesn't look so pleasant. It was dreary and the ground was covered in snow and the roads were looked mushy and gross. I thought Kansas City's trees were burned because the trees had no leaves. I could not help but ask what happened to the trees without leaves. This was my introduction to education about the four seasons in the Midwest.

As I stepped down on the seminary campus, I saw a pile of snow on the ground. I touched the snow to see what it felt like. I said, "It's like ice."

My host smiled at me and said, "Yes. It is ice."

They took me to the Scheoukolf building, where I would be staying. It was spring break and the school was so quiet. I was treated very well. They showed me around. The grocery store was within walking distance. Everything I saw looked so fascinating, new, and special. For the first time, I felt like I was living in a nice hotel. Breakfast, lunch, and dinner were all prearranged.

Those who left the campus invited me for meals. The third day I was on my own. I walked to the Kroger grocery store. It was cold, but I managed because someone gave me a warm coat. I was amazed that the food was so cheap. I could buy the chicken liver and gizzard by the cents, and that included ice cream. These items were so expensive at home, so I bought the familiar things I could carry and had been longing to eat, including rice. That day I had a good feast. Since I was alone, there were plenty of leftovers from my first meal, so I had to eat again the liver and gizzard. Soon enough I got sick of the smell and taste of it. That was my first and last time buying those foods.

On my first day of school, I met my roommate, Reverend Dave Jacob from Nebraska. I was well dressed as I went to the classroom. I noticed some students who came in. They were wearing very casual clothes, and I could not tell who the professor was among the students. It was obvious that I was the only one dressed up. Someone thought I was a guest speaker. At lunchtime, we all went to the dining facility. I was introduced as a new foreign student, and that's when I found out that it was the whole student body that donated the money for my airfare to come to the United States.

I thanked the whole student body and Reverend Paul Akin, who led the student body to raise the money for my coming to the United States. Reverend Ken Green introduced himself, and we became very good friends. He was single and serving a two-point charge, (aka: two-churches in one area under the leadership of one pastor) at Missouri at that time. He invited me to preach at his church. After I preached, they collected more than $250 and offered it to me. I was so thrilled to receive that much. That was already more than a year's salary for a pastor like me in the Philippines. The news got around quickly. Students started to invite me to their churches to preach. The school decided that anybody who invited me to preach should give their offering directly to the school, and this money would be set aside for me in case I needed something, such as health insurance, school and emergency needs, etc.

Nobody knew about my wife until I started showing her picture to my fellow seminarians. The seminary registrar found out about this and called me to his office. I told him I met this woman, Aleta Corre, after I started processing my papers for the United States. I told him we were in love and decided to get married a week before my flight. The school plainly told me that there was no way they could bring my wife to join me in the United States. Meanwhile, Reverend Michael White, a very friendly student, approached me and invited me to his church to speak. Amazingly, he announced to his church that I was married and told his church that they needed to help me bring my wife to the States. I didn't have any idea how he would do it, but I prayed fervently for their good intentions and asked God to make it happen.

My acquaintances also started to grow. The school was trying to prove that my speaking engagements were not enough to sustain my schooling and daily expenses. I needed a job with regular income. A student who was about to graduate told me that he was leaving his internship job and janitorial work at Old Mission United Methodist Church in Shawnee Mission, Kansas. I was offered the job, and I accepted it.

The news spread quickly, and some members of the church were trying to reach and befriend me. However, the job was not available until after summer. Meanwhile, I continued to write my wife and put cash in every letter I mailed. I sent ten, twenty, or thirty dollars at most. This was already a great help for her to meet her daily needs and her family's needs. I heard that my parents had been bringing some agricultural products whenever they went to visit Leth.

I met Pete Borel, president of Borel Jewelry in Kansas City. He was an active member of the church where I would be going and also an active member of the businessmen's Charismatic Movement. He took me to different Charismatic Worship services as well as to the Old Mission UMC Men's Bible study. As my acquaintances grew, many started to pray and express support for my getting my wife to join me in the States.

Meanwhile, a disturbing report came from the Board of Ordained Ministry of the Middle Philippine Annual Conference (MidPAC), headed by Dr. Emerito Nacpil. The letter indicated that I was AWOL, without the consent of the Board of Ordained Ministry. Since I was no longer endorsed by the church, it was their understanding that the seminary would send me back home. The news reached my parents and friends that soon I would come back because I was AWOL. I was told that Dr. Nacpil even said at the conference that I was not really called to the ministry but was taking advantage of a schooling opportunity. The school registrar told me that MidPAC canceled my membership and would send me back to the Philippines.

Dr B. Rathjen was the new registrar of the seminary. He looked at my personal file and saw the recommendation of Reverend Dr. Jose Gamboa Jr., the former secretary of the MidPAC Board of Ordained Ministry. The registrar sensed that there were some factions and I was caught in the middle. He asked me what my desire was since I no longer belonged to any denomination. I told him I dreamed of becoming a preacher of Christ's gospel. He called one of the district superintendents of the Kansas East Conference to help me restore the process of attaining my conference membership.

The restoration of my membership to the Kansas East Conference gave me a favorable award. My scholarship was paid, I was given a book allowance, and my health insurance was paid in full. I thought what the MidPAC did to me was a curse, but in the end it was a great blessing in my favor. What a blessing. God must have been watching me closely with all his grace and favor. My parents were hardened by MidPAC's unkind decision. However, I wrote my family back and told them not to be disappointed, because their decision became a blessing on my part. I told them I now belonged to the Kansas East Conference, here in Kansas.

When summer came, I expressed my desire to find a summer job to save for my schooling and at the same time for my wife's airfare. Pete Borel happened to be a very influential man and had many business acquaintances. He introduced me to the head of Immigration and Naturalization, someone who also happened to be a member of the Old Mission UMC. I was given several forms to fill out and instructed that I needed to petition my wife under the student visa.

The Grain Valley UMC, served by Reverend Michael White, took the initiative to fill out the form petitioning the sponsor to bring my wife to the States. I had to raise money for a round-trip ticket before Immigration and Naturalization Services could give my wife a visa. With the help and support of friends, the sponsoring church of Grain

Valley UMC, and guaranteed monthly income from the Old Mission UMC, my wife's approval to come to the States came smoothly.

My wife joined me in Kansas City several weeks prior to the start of classes. We stayed in Scheoukolf until we moved to our new home, the basement of the Old Mission UMC, Shawnee Mission. It was one bedroom with a nice kitchen and lounge. Grain Valley gave us kitchen equipment, utensils, a set of plates, bedding, and canned goods to help us get started. Old Mission UMC members also gave us some necessities.

Pete Borel had a newly converted Jewish friend who had an extra old car, a Rambler station wagon, which was still running well and he gave to me for free. Grandpa Roy and Mama Loretta had no kids, and they adopted us as their own. We got settled quickly through the help of these loving church people. I strongly felt God's presence and that he was working in our favor.

The job was not that bad. I opened the church early in the morning, cleaned up after the day care center and church office every day, cleaned the church on Monday and Saturday, and closed the church at night. I was there supposedly as an intern. I think that was just a title, because the truth was that I worked mainly as an assistant to the janitor. Leth was so helpful to me. I always came home with heavy schoolwork and reading. My job became a lot easier with her help.

During the day she helped at the office until they made her work in a paying job. Soon enough we had a predictable monthly income. After assessing our income, we figured out what we could afford if she continued her master's degree at the University of Missouri, Kansas City. She enrolled, and after two and a half years, she finished her master's degree in educational elementary administration.

Student pastors were all encouraged to work in the institutional environment or parish setting prior to seminary graduation. I had to take a weekend job as a youth pastor in Sedalia, Missouri. I left early on Saturday morning and stayed there until Sunday. I also took basic and advanced clinical pastoral education (CPE) courses at Trinity Lutheran Hospital under the leadership of Chaplain Carlson, CPE supervisor.

Prior to our graduation, Leth gave birth to our first child, our daughter, Amihan Robin Valdez. She was born on December 24, 1975, at Menorah Hospital in Kansas City. That was a hard night for me, because I was working at the church shoveling snow in preparation for the Christmas Eve services while my wife was in labor. On the other hand, it was a great week because it was a school break and I had no schoolwork to worry about. I considered this another one of God's blessings, because our child came as our special Christmas gift. She came at the right time, when I could spend time with her and her mother for another week before classes resumed.

Graduation month finally came. Leth graduated from the University of Missouri, Kansas City, and I graduated from Saint Paul School of Theology, Kansas City, with a Master of Divinity degree. Friends and acquaintances congratulated us. They were amazed at how well we planned. Amy was born during Christmas break in 1975, and Leth and I both graduated with master's degrees during the summer of 1976. Now that we were both finished with our degrees, it was about time to move again and serve a local church.

Chapter 4

First Parish and Travel

The Kansas East Conference put me in a two-point charge (AKA: two-churches assigned to one pastor.) in Fort Scott Kansas: the former Evangelical United Brethren (EUB) Church and the Hiattville United Methodist Church. Reverend Ken Green, a close friend, loaned me his car to pull a small U-Haul loaded with our household goods. Our old Rambler was about to give up. A member of our new church helped us find another used car, newer than our current car. This time it was a green Hornet.

There were two United Methodist churches in Fort Scott. The small church was the former EUB, and the other larger church was the First United Methodist Church. Hiattville UMC was located in a rural setting. It was probably less than ten miles from Fort Scott. The church membership I was serving in town was mostly elderly but financially stable. The Hiattville UMC membership was mostly farmers and young adults in their late twenties. There were very few elderly. We could really relate to these young families, because we were in the same stage of life. Many of them had children about the same age as our daughter, Amy.

While in Fort Scott, Leth seemed to know how to deal with the church members. She started to introduce the members to Amy by calling them "Grandma" or "Grandpa." The elderly seemed to like it, and they started adopting Amy as their grandkid and us as a part of their family. These relationships brought us close, as if we found not just a church to lead but a close family of our own. In every aspect of my work, all kinds of church activities and events, Leth supported me, sometimes doing some of my work for me. Someone said he was so lucky because he felt like he had two clergies, except that one was unpaid. So often I attributed the growth of our church to Leth because of her love of Christ and her sincere commitment to help the church grow spiritually and through membership.

In spite of the wonderful relationship we had with the church, Leth and I were getting homesick. I indicated to my bishop our desire to go home and to transfer me to the Philippines. Bishop Dixon, the resident bishop of the Kansas East Conference, told me that he could transfer me if I so desired. However, he also told me that if things didn't work, Kansas East Conference was my home conference and I was always welcome if I ever wanted to come back.

The desire to go home became stronger. We had not seen our birth country since we left for school. We announced that we were coming home. The Middle Philippine Annual Conference wanted me back because, they said, I really belonged to them. I was disturbed by their claim since they abandoned me when I left the country. I told them I belonged to Kansas East Conference and I wanted my bishop to transfer me, not to MidPAC, but to the Philippine Annual Conference (PAC).

Bishop Paul Locke Granadosin, resident bishop of the PAC, accepted me in his episcopal area. He appointed me to the Malabon North United Methodist Church in Malabon, Metro Manila, Philippines. The whole family was so excited by this move. Furthermore, it was a lot closer to Leth's family. Leth and I loved to travel. Even when Amy was newly born, we were always traveling whenever we could to see the country. Since we had not seen Europe, we decided to travel via the Atlantic prior to going back to the Philippines.

We flew from Kansas City to London, then Paris, Rome, Athens, Tel-Aviv, Jerusalem, and several other cities in Israel. We went on to Baghdad, Bangkok, Hong Kong, Kowloon, and finally, back to Manila. We visited tourist spots in every city in which we landed. It was an exhilarating, educational, and exciting experience. In the States, Amy was not exposed to many Filipinos, so she called every Filipino friend we had "Uncle" and "Auntie." When we reached London, we met some Filipinos and they started talking to us. Amy said, "There are some uncles and aunties here too." When we reached Bangkok, Amy said, "Mom, there are so many uncles and aunties here." And when we reached the Philippines, she said, "Dad, all people here are uncles and aunties." And when we introduced her to her real grandmas and grandpas (our parents), Amy refused to accept them, saying, "My grandmas and grandpas are white, not like them."

In London, as we were riding in the double-decker bus, the conductor was collecting money. The conductor and a female passenger were arguing with each other. The passenger insisted that she had paid the conductor, saying, "I swear! I swear!" The conductor, on the other hand, was getting upset, saying that she had not paid at all. Everybody were so quiet, listening to the argument. The passenger kept on saying, "I swear! I swear!" The conductor finally gave up arguing, and there was a long silence until Amy perked up and said out loud, "I swear! I swear!" Amy's voice instigated a roar of laughter inside the bus while Leth and I were melting from embarrassment.

In Israel, we decided to stay longer to see the entire country. We rented a car from the Tel Aviv airport. We studied the route to Jerusalem, Bethlehem, Jericho, etc., to see some historic places where Jesus had been. On our way to Jerusalem, all edges of the big highways seemed surrounded by soldiers with heavy guns and ammunition. They inspected our luggage to see what we had. It was annoying but we managed. Then three soldiers stopped us. They were hitchhiking. They wanted to ride with us until Jerusalem. That gave us a freedom from searches up to Jerusalem. We learned from these soldiers that the airport in Tel Aviv had been bombed by some Japanese rebels. Since we looked Japanese because of our complexion, we could have been potential suspects. They apologized for something they could not help.

We endured these inspections throughout Israel. Leth and I were so fascinated by how history and tradition evolved in this very rich country where Jesus walked and grew. The experience was very educational and awakening. It was sad in many ways, because most of the historic locations were already highly commercialized, though some of it had been carefully preserved for future generations.

We did not stay long in Baghdad because of the heat. However, when we reached Bangkok, we had the chance to see cultural shows and ride on an elephant. Those were good treats for all of us, especially Amy.

Our money went further in this third-world country. I was so amazed by how powerful the dollar was in third-world countries, even in Europe at that time. Hong Kong was a good one too. It was considered the shopping center of Asia. I saw several Japanese visit Hong Kong to go shopping. Most of the products were less expensive in Hong Kong than in Japan. Isn't that strange?

Chapter 5

The Manila Challenges

Finally, we arrived in Manila. So much had changed since we left: more people, more transportation, and more pollution. But it was so nice to be back home. Relatives and friends came to meet us at the airport. We moved right away to our new parsonage. There were welcome parties at Leth's home, our new home, and our new church. As usual, the church was full on my first Sunday. Perhaps many members wanted to hear this new preacher. I preached one of the most well-rehearsed sermons I had ever done before. I think I made a very good first impression, because the church members came back and they brought members who had not been active with them and the Malabon North United Methodist Church was packed.

As I engaged with the life of our church members and the injustices going on in the country, I could not help but study and learn more about the poverty and oppression caused by the authorities who were in power. Most of the Bible studies topics were always unavoidably about socioeconomic injustices. Even in my sermon, I could not help but touch on the inhumane issues that affected the life of the Filipino people. Soon enough, I was contacted by clergy associations that were actively working with people about the human struggles for justice.

Some people came to the parsonage hungry, and sometimes we had to feed them. Some members were nice enough to share food with us. My salary as a pastor was standard and decent for the area, but it was almost not enough for our basic needs, like food. We could not save any money. I enjoyed what I was doing, but Leth was so concerned about our financial status and always scared for my physical well-being. I had been warned by some members that there were military spies listening to my sermons who thought my message was subversive.

Leth and I continued to argue a lot about financial matters. My income barely covered our basic needs. We were sure that we could never afford to get sick. Leth also overheard that authorities may not hurt me, but they used families to get what they wanted. Fears overcame her, and she decided to go back to the States with Amy. I resisted the idea, but I could not stop her. She made up her mind. She even told me, "I wish, if they kill you, they do it quickly and make sure you're dead. I would hate to see you get hurt and be paralyzed forever. Then you will be dependent on others, and you won't like that."

I knew my marriage was about to disintegrate. Leth knew I could not sleep. She gave me the silent treatment for several days, which bothered me more. One night she surprised me by kissing and hugging me. She said, "You know, I love you so much and I am doing this for our future." Her words and hug almost melted me down. It was a good feeling and a huge relief. She said, "I am going to the States to work and will send you some money so you can do what you enjoy." I felt like she blessed me, and I too must bless her plans. Leth and Amy flew back to the States.

Now I had more freedom. I became more active in people's lives under the leadership of an ecumenical group of clergies. I had a great congregation; most of them were very loving and supportive. The church was very active, and most members were very creative, talented, and motivated. This made my ministry a lot easier.

However, no matter how you try to do a good job, there are always some small groups that create some challenges. Unfortunately, there were two members who were considered elders of the church, and they had been Sunday school teachers for a long time. When I attended Sunday school, they asked my opinion about Jesus Christ as God. I gave them an indirect answer that I learned from the seminary. I gave them the traditional answer as well as the counter-traditional answer to the godship of Jesus Christ. "There is no question about Jesus Christ, the Son of God," I said. "However, there is a big difference between 'Jesus is God' and the 'Son of God.' Unfortunately, Jesus never said, 'I am

God,' except some verses in the Scripture that seem to imply He was. So even now, it remains a controversy."

This statement was a big issue for them, and this group started to spread the rumor that I didn't believe in Jesus Christ as God. They started boycotting the church and telling members that it was wrong to listen to a preacher who didn't believe Jesus Christ was God. They seemed to bark so loud, but they were not getting much attention. So they reported me to the bishop and convinced him that we must have a dialogue or confrontation because I was teaching doctrine that was not in line with the doctrine of the United Methodist Church.

The bishop listened to both sides. After a while, the bishop asked me to leave so that he could talk to the group. Once the bishop was done talking to the group, he talked to me. He understood my position and the scholarly discourse. I thought he would discourage me from doctrinal teaching, but he was supportive instead. Since the bishop did not give me a disciplinary action, as the other party anticipated, the following week there was a rumor that the bishop was accused of being weak and had no determination. I lost some members in my congregation, but at least I heard that they went to another church. It was a very sad situation.

The freedom to do what I wanted was great. I was itching to teach at the university and was given the chance to do it. I taught two courses—Christian ethics and ethics—at Philippine Christian University. It was a tremendous joy teaching college students who were eager to learn. As I taught, I thought I learned more from them than they learned from me. I loved the interaction with my students and the opportunity to help them apply ethical issues to the present condition of the country. I never thought of myself as subversive, but some thought my teaching and my message had elements of subversion. Whatever they thought, I knew well in my heart that I was just preaching what I believed was the gospel of Jesus Christ, my Lord.

Leth invited me to take a vacation in the States. Amy and Leth must have been missing me. Perhaps it would be a good break for me, so I accepted the offer. I left for a two- to three-week vacation to see my family. Amy and Leth were living in a very small apartment next door to Kuya Eming's apartment. I was happy indeed when I saw my family, but my heart was about to crush when my little girl did not recognize me, especially when she pointed to my picture and said, "That's my daddy." I hugged her so tightly and could not control my tears. I told her, "I'm your dad."

Kuya Eming and his wife, Ate Lucy, were considerate enough to take Amy with them for the whole night to give Leth and me some privacy. It was a joyous, passionate reunion, indeed. Leth woke up early because she had to go to work. I spent my time with Amy and Ate Lucy. At lunch break, Kuya Eming came home and ate with us. Ate Lucy and Kuya Eming briefed me that day about my family's situation. They admired Leth's commitment and dedication to her family. She had lots of hardship in Fort Scott, where she went first. The pastor who preceded me felt insecure by her presence, because our former members loved her and she got so much affection. Her presence seemed threatening, and it was considered unethical for a pastor's family to come back from where they left.

Leth left Fort Scott and worked in Nevada, Missouri, where she met a Filipino family. She worked full-time, and Amy had difficulty adjusting to moving from one place to another and having a different babysitter. When Kuya Eming moved from the East Coast to Saint Joseph, Missouri, they all decided to stay close together. Amy then was more stable, and Leth felt more secure close to them. She worked hard to support, not just themselves, but also me in the Philippines.

The apartment was just one small room with a hideaway bed. The bedroom and kitchen were all together, and the restroom and shower were in a separate space. Most people who lived there were single and elderly, and Amy was the only child in that building. The area was not really suitable for kids, but that was where my family was living. Kuya Eming told me, "I can understand the cause you are fighting for. And it is a great cause, and your wife seems supportive of that. However, I want you to think about this. If something happens to you, your family will be the ones who will step up and take care of you. When your career is over, your family will be responsible for taking care of you. The people you try to help will surely appreciate what you have done for them. They might take care of you for a little while, but will they be there for you forever? Only your family, who loves you, can really take care of you. Everything goes back to the family. So, Mel, love your family the way they love you."

I thought about it for a long time. When I got back to my wife and my daughter's apartment, I looked at what they had and burst into tears, like a child. Was I that selfish? Was preaching the gospel more important to me than my family? Was it my wife's fault for leaving me? Could she not stand the pressure I was under? Was it fair to choose between preaching the gospel in my homeland, where I felt personally productive, and my own family who disagreed with me? What about that innocent little child, Amy? She was torn between two people who had different ideas of what was good for her, or good for us. Now, what was it?

Since Leth was so busy working to make a living, I got bored while waiting for my last day of vacation. Meanwhile, I got an extra job to make some money. I never told the employer that I was a degree holder and a professional clergy. However, the supervisor noticed that I had the ability to lead and supervise. Amazingly, I was offered several attractive administrative jobs, but I told them I was just killing time and my vacation was about over. Finally, my vacation was over and it was time to go back to the Philippines, the country I called home. I had mixed emotions about leaving my family, but I was so excited to get back to my real work.

When I got back to the Philippines, I immediately got back to work. However, every night I was haunted by mixed emotions about my ministry and my family. It became like a ritual for me to look at my wife and my daughter's picture before I went to bed. Every night was emotional and stressful, as I thought about my family. But when the next day came, the work kept me distracted. I was always busy and had no time to think of the family.

One day, Kuya Eming wrote me an urgent letter, telling me that my wife was sick, Amy was so confused, and I must come as soon as possible. This news distressed me so badly, and without hesitation I made the decision to be with my family. The Pastor-Parish Relations

Committee of the church, including the bishop, gave me the blessing to leave the country as soon as possible. Friends, church members, and families were so supportive of me. All the papers and documents needed to go back to the States were filed smoothly. And I was on my way to the United States.

Chapter 6

Looking for Home State

I joined my family in the States and immediately felt like I had to move them out of the Midwest. I wanted to stay where there were more Filipinos, where it was warm, where there wasn't any snow. California was clear in my mind. I called my mother's cousin, Auntie Lina Romasanta, and asked if I could stay with them for a while until I found a job in LA. Since her husband was retired from the US Navy, she told me he had plenty of time to help me find a job. That was very assuring, and I felt encouraged that all things would go well in California.

It was snowing in Saint Joseph, Missouri, when I left for California. I left Leth and Amy and promised them that they would follow me as soon as I found a job and a place to stay. That early morning, I drove my wife's fifteen-year-old Ford Galaxy. I was nervous about the move with that old car, but I was hopeful that things would get better with the help and grace of God.

I traveled from Missouri down to southern Oklahoma and then Texas, hoping it would be warmer and the traveling would be smooth. I was wrong. Between Oklahoma and Texas I had to travel on icy roads and saw several cars and trucks veer off the road and into a ditch. It was a scary journey, but I managed. When I reached Arizona, it was already dark. I was determined to travel all night long until I got tired. Unfortunately, there was another storm that hit. It was a sandstorm. It was so dark that night. All I saw was a storm of sand-like rain hitting my car. The paved road was no longer visible, except for the curve of ditches. I stayed in the middle of the road to avoid the ditch. Fortunately, there was a semi in front of me. I hoped I could keep up with it by following its tracks, but the sand was just so thick that I had almost zero visibility. I did not sleep that night. Instead I kept driving until morning, when that terrible sandstorm had passed.

My car started to sound funny. I needed to find an auto service nearby to check my car. Luckily, one gas station was open and had a mechanic. He said the engine air filter was clogged with sand. Furthermore, the tires were about to give up. He found several soft bulges in each side of the tires, which were ready to explode at any time. The radiator pipe was leaking. It was a mess. At that time I really learned to value credit cards, since I had limited cash. After almost half a day, I was back on the road again. Before reaching the California border, another snowstorm hit me on my way around the mountains. The snow was so thick that many vehicles had to stop while they were clearing the road.

The travel was a nightmare. I finally got going down the mountain and started seeing the beautiful towns of California until I reached my destination. The weather was nice—neither too cold nor hot, almost perfect. The traffic was heavy, but it did not bother me at all. I had just come from the Philippines, where the heavy traffic was the worst. California traffic was not that bad. As I reached Carson City, Uncle Romy Romasanta was already expecting me. It was a good reunion since I had not seen them for so long. Uncle Romy told me, "If you are not choosy, you'll get a job quickly."

He was right. That day, as I went to every industrial complex office in the nearby area and applied for a job, one of the electronic companies took me in with their simple mathematical test. The test was so simple and seemed designed for a grade-schooler. It was so simple that I scored 100 percent. I was assigned to shipping and handling. The job was so easy and boring, but it helped me get my family from Missouri to California. Leth and Amy traveled by bus.

Leth did not wait too long to get settled. Instead, she went to find a job herself. She applied for a county clerk position in Los Angeles and got the job quickly. Since I was so bored and the job was less challenging, I too started to look for a better job with higher pay. I found a job at the same place as Leth. I served as a county clerk map reader. I helped people find on the county map the property lots they were buying. I found it as a challenging job. It worked in our favor since we only had one car. It was also a perfect arrangement for our daughter, Amy. The child care center happened to be just a few blocks from where we worked.

As Leth started feeling comfortable, I was feeling empty inside. The salary and benefits were good, but my desire to go back to parish ministry was getting stronger and stronger. The California United Methodist Church Conference year was just around the corner. I started inquiring about the appointment process for a pastor in the United Methodist Church. I applied through the help of some Filipino clergy and laity. I was told to stand by since they had to appoint all their clergies first who belong to the California UMC Conference.

I knew I would get a church. I prayed, and it seemed like God answered my prayers. It might not have been what I had in mind, but it was where God needed me to be. Kuya Eming called to ask me to join him in Iowa since that state didn't have Filipino clergy, except Reverend Berbano. Iowa at that time had a shortage of pastors. I said I would consider the idea; however, I was prepared to go to California since I was not too excited about cold weather and snow. I prayed to God that whoever would open the door first, it would be God's will. Early on a Saturday in June, Iowa called to see if I would be interested in considering pastoring two churches in the Spencer District of the Iowa Conference. I was sure that was the answer to my prayers, and without any hesitation, I accepted it.

The following day, early Sunday morning, a district superintendent from California Conference asked me if I was willing to serve in Pasadena, California. The offer made me realize that I would rather stay in California than Iowa, but I had to honor Iowa since I had already made a commitment to them. I also promised God that whoever opened the door first would be God's plan for me. My wife did not want to move to a cold state since we had just come from there that same year. Fortunately, she gave in. We both knew we prayed for the first opening and considered it the will of God for us. We had to explain to the caller from California how much we appreciated the offer, but we had to honor Iowa.

We immediately started packing again. We had to give away all large items we had just bought to make the move easier. Amy was so confused, but she too was thrilled because we were going to be united again with the Tabelismas, the only relatives Amy knew. A Filipino pastor, a newly seminary graduate, and a close friend of mine, Reverend Hemesias Aris, decided to ride along with us as we traveled to Iowa. We had to buy a new car, an LTD Ford, which was more reliable than our old car. The car was well packed with our load.

We had a week to travel before I had to start my pastorate work. Since we had not seen much of the West Coast, we decided to travel leisurely, enjoy the ride, and stop at some areas of interest. We packed a family tent for camping, which saved us money from expensive hotels. Our first stop was in Las Vegas, Nevada. We found a nice camping area close to the city. Reverend Hemie Aris and I decided to see Las Vegas at night. We both were anxious to see the area without inhibition since nobody knew who we were and would identify us as clergy of the United Methodist Church. Both of us had five dollars to spend for our entertainment, either on a movie or in the slot machines. We went to the big casinos and saw many people playing the slot machines.

Rather than going to the movie, we were intent on having the fun of those who were winning at the slot machines. But I was scared of all the talk I was hearing that I could become easily addicted once I started playing. To avoid that addiction, we decided to spend the money, which would have been used on a movie, on the slot machines. We would not add any more, whether or not we were winning. It was one way, I supposed, to justify in our mind that we did not gamble. We just spent time entertaining ourselves.

We went to the cashier and changed our ten dollars into quarters. The money went to the slots so fast that our fun was almost quickly over. Suddenly, one of us had a good strike and, lo and behold, we started filling up our coin baskets with plenty of winnings. We were winning, and amazingly we had doubled and then tripled our money. We decided to use all the coins we had until they were gone. After a long night of fun, I could not believe we also lost all the money we had. We left the casino late that night but were laughing and thrilled by the fun. We could not believe our coins lasted that long. That experience made me understand how gambling could become easily addictive.

The next day we woke up late, and after breakfast we started packing our tent again. We left Las Vegas with lots of stories to tell. Now we were heading to Utah. We stopped to see the Mormon Cathedral and took a tour. We also stopped to see the splendor and beauty of Bryce Canyon. And as we reached Colorado, we encountered lots of snow in the mountainous state that spoiled our plan to enjoy the rocky mountain high of Colorado.

We even encountered a fallen rock on our way that I swerved to avoid it. It was nighttime when suddenly I saw the rock in the middle of the road. My immediate reaction was to drive over the rock, hoping my car was high enough to avoid hitting it. But I was wrong! The rock was big enough to jerk our car so hard that I thought it damaged the whole bottom of the new car, including the gas tank. Amazingly it was okay in spite of the big dent I saw underneath the car.

We reached the valley of Nebraska, and then the next state was finally Iowa, the corn state. The whole trip was tiring but great. We had to get used to the roads of Iowa since we came from a big, crowded city. The names of the roads were quite different from those in the cities. The county road was named by letter and number together, such as F1. There was a lot of distance between road signs. Sometimes we were not sure whether we were still on the right route. When we finally located where we were supposed to be going, we saw the Tabelismas and stayed with them to get a feel for the new state, which soon would serve as my residence—our new home state of Iowa!

Chapter 7

The Corn State Ministry

T he parsonage was a colonial home. The hardwood floors and doors were solid and old. It looked good, as far as I was concerned. This was our first time in a big parsonage. It was more than enough for the three of us. The office was already in the parsonage, and the kitchen was big, perfect for Leth to entertain guests and visitors. Our arrival in summertime was great because some church members prepared the parsonage vegetable garden, and some of it was ready for us to harvest. We felt very welcomed, and Leth and Amy were overwhelmed with the hospitality. Yes, we were now in Iowa, the corn state.

Harold Devaul and his wife came and gave us a tour around the town. The town was small, with a little more than five hundred people. They fell in love with our daughter and adopted her as their honorary grandchild immediately. Since we did not have much to furnish the house, members of both United Methodist churches of Inwood and Lester, Iowa showered us with furniture and dishes. These two towns were in northwest corner of Iowa. Inwood was probably five miles from the South Dakota state line, while Lester was just three miles from the Minnesota state line. We were the only people of color in the area until the community started to sponsor a refugee family from Vietnam.

It happened that the principal and the superintendent of the community school were members of our church. They helped Leth find a teaching job at the school that kept her busy while I was busy with the two churches. The Inwood church membership was made up of mostly elderly people, but had a few young adults. Financially, it was a stable church and larger in membership. The second congregation was smaller but with lots of young couples and children. These two joined together and formed a decent appointment that met the minimum wage for clergy required by the Iowa Conference of The United Methodist Church.

The community was small, but everyone was proud of their heritage. There was a bank, post office, small hardware store, park, café, big commercial barn where farmers sold and stored their harvest, barbershop, etc. It was a good town where you could get most of your basic needs. Perhaps the biggest city in the area was Sioux Falls, South Dakota, which was around fifteen miles. This was the city where people would go to spend their money.

During my first month in Inwood, I decided to visit the barbershop and to start getting to know the people in the community. The barber was not that busy, and I was his first customer. He started the conversation and asked me if I was new in town. Of course, I was, so I answered him affirmatively. Then he continued to ask me more questions, trying to get to know me more. "Where do you work?" he asked.

I said, "I work at the First United Methodist Church here in Inwood."

To my surprise, he said, "Oh, are you the new janitor?"

I just smiled when Harold Devaul came in and said, "Good morning, Pastor. So you met our new pastor in our church."

The barber apologized for thinking I was the janitor of the church.

The whole town had only two ethnic minority families, the Vietnamese refugees and us. Since the community was not exposed to many people of color, sometimes they thought we were the refugees. As I got involved in many public activities and many meetings of the community clergies, businessmen, and other organizations, people started to know me more and more. Since our church was in the center of the town, it was used for the weekly luncheon of the Kiwanis, cooked by the church ladies in town. These activities helped me get to know many community leaders and also helped our church in our outreach ministries.

It was on April 1, 1980, that our second child was born. The night before his birth, Leth woke up and said, "Mel, my water broke."

I said, "Are you sure? It may be urine! Try to smell it first."

Well, she did. "It doesn't smell like urine" was her remark.

We woke up Amy and packed all the necessary things I could think Leth might need if she stayed in the hospital. I took her to Rock Valley Hospital in the town next to Inwood, the closest hospital in the area. I called the pastor of Rock Valley UMC, Reverend David Waterman, and his wife and asked them to take care of Amy. Leth continued to expel water slowly. They had to cut the opening for the baby to come out. Otherwise the baby could die due to a lack of water inside Leth's womb.

It was midmorning when the baby finally arrived. We had to think of a Filipino name and listed all we could think of. After all the lists of names, we finally agreed to name him Magdiwang Ruel Valdez. Magdiwang means "celebration." "Ruel" was the name of one of a college friend at Philippine Wesleyan College. We worried at first when our son opened only one eye, but the doctor, a native of Thailand, assured us that he was all right. He had one sleepy eye, but it could be corrected with cosmetic surgery at a later date.

We were very happy to announce to our church members that we had a newly born son, but no one believed me because it happened on April Fools' Day. They thought I was just fooling around. So they asked Amy. Amy confirmed that she had a baby brother. It was only then that they believed me and congratulated me. Harold Devaul came to see our son and asked his name. When I told him his name, he had trouble pronouncing it. He said, "I'll just call him Randy." He looked at Magdiwang and said, "Poor boy! This boy will hate you for naming him that when he grows up … whatever. Right, Randy?"

I thought that he might be right. So then we started calling Magdiwang Diwang. Diwang means "idea" or "concept." Well, it was too late to change. His name was already registered. Magdiwang and Diwang were still good Filipino names.

That year the General United Methodist Church stressed ethnic minority inclusiveness. Since there were few minorities in the Iowa Conference, we were given special attention. It was at that time that I was elected by the Jurisdictional Conference of the UMC for the first time to serve as a director of the General Board of Global Ministries. It was an exciting journey for me, because it gave me the big picture of how the United Methodist Church worked in the mission in the global arena. I was assigned to serve in the Education and Cultivation Division, the Crusade Scholarship Division, and the World Division. New York City was the location of the main headquarters for the General Board of Global Ministry.

To serve in all these capacities, I did not realize that I too must serve at the conference level. I spent lots of time traveling and attending meetings and conferences, at the district, state, and general levels. I was so thrilled with the vast education about the greatness of Methodism, our connectional church. Since I was so busy traveling and obviously out of sight, this created some problems for members of our two local churches. The Inwood UMC raised the issue of why they were paying a pastor who was always gone. Some members who understood the connectional church system tried to explain how they as a local church benefited from understanding the broad and global mission work of the church.

The bickering among the members created a small faction that turned into a personal, and perhaps racial, issue. This started to bother me. I overheard some comments, like "Why did the United Methodist Church assign colored people in the white churches?" and "I don't understand him at all when he preaches!" and "He is better off going back to where he came from and serving his own people" and finally "He is not serving our church; he is always in Des Moines or in New York." (Des Moines and New York denoted the headquarters of UMC in Iowa and the national elite of the UMC board of mission.)

My discomfort and stress started to affect me and my performance. I had to talk to the district superintendent (DS). The DS had to come for a special church conference. He met first the Pastor-Parish Relations Committee. He explained to them the meaning of a connectional church and the importance of my involvement in the district, annual, and general level of our connectional church. The Pastor-Parish Relations Committee expressed their support for me. The church conference followed, and then only two or three families were dissatisfied with the connectional system and threatened to leave the church. The discussion went also into a personal dissatisfaction with having an ethnic minority pastor in a white congregation.

After the session, I was in deep distress, and the DS felt he had to move me after I finished my term that year. The majority of the members were very supportive of my ministry. Members sensed the discomfort I had, and many of the church members verbally expressed their support of my ministry. One of the most outspoken people who was supportive of my ministry was the principal, Don Nelson. Don later became a successful lay pastor of the Iowa Annual Conference. Reverend Don Nelson became the pastor of Lester United Methodist Church, the church that once was my appointment under the Inwood-Lester charge. Lester UMC became the fastest growing small church in Iowa, and perhaps in the country.

The church was growing in spite of the local crisis we had and my continuous involvement in the connectional church. After the Iowa Conference, the bishop moved me to Galva-Silver Creek UMC. Prior to my arrival, the DS, who was aware of the problem I had from the previous church, told the Pastor-Parish Relations Committee about my involvement in the global and conference level of the connectional church. This helped to prevent a similar problem with the new churches. Fortunately, these two churches were much involved in local, national, and global missions. I was very welcomed, and many of the church members were anxious to hear from me about what was going on in our mission.

Leth, in all of these years since I started my parish ministries in the States, had always helped me and was very much involved in the life of the church. Oftentimes members thought Leth should be paid for what she did. They felt like they had a clergy couple. It helped me a lot when I was traveling and having meeting or conferences. At one time, I was stranded in Chicago one Saturday night when my airline did not make it through due to bad weather. Leth went ahead and led the Sunday worship service and read my sermon to the congregation. She did it very professionally, and many church members applauded her leadership. Truly, I attribute many of my successes in the ministry to her commitment to the church and her charisma while working with church members.

At Silver Creek, we had a church member who happened to be an elected state senator of Iowa, Wayne Bennett. Wayne invited me to open the prayer before the House of Representatives and the Senate to open their sessions. It was a good and humbling experience for me. I did not expect remuneration, but to my surprise they paid me seventy-five dollars for my short prayer. I bragged to my friends that my less-than-a-minute prayer cost that much. Another humbling experience was that during my ministry at Galva-Silver Creek, two people felt the call to serve God in the local church and went on to seminary and then their own churches. Both of them attributed their calling to my ministries. The same was true for Don Nelson from Inwood. He claimed that his interest in the ministry started at the time of my presence at the Inwood UMC. His wife and my wife became very close friends, and up to this day we try to stay connected with them.

Our Galva-Silver Creek experiences were very rewarding. It was at that time that I was already ready to move again for a change. Our kids were in grade school already, and I wanted them to go to school close to us and to a city where there were plenty of children's activities. North Liberty and Tiffin United Methodist, a another two-church appointment, opened up. These two churches were both bedroom communities for Iowa City, Iowa, the former location of the capital city for the state of Iowa.

Iowa City was the home of the University of Iowa, the well-known Hawkeyes. I knew this would be a perfect place for my kids to grow and go to school. The parsonage was in North Liberty. The town was small, but it was close enough to Iowa City so that we could go and get almost anything that we needed. The grade school was almost in our backyard. Amy and Diwang walked to school every day.

Amy went to Coralville for middle school. She got involved in advanced ballet and also had the opportunity to teach young kids in our church. She choreographed some ballet using spiritual music and used it for interpretative dance through worship. Diwang and Amy also got involved in arts, and their works won some medals for exhibits at Hancher Auditorium. Diwang got involved in soccer, and he played the violin. The whole family got involved in studying tae kwon do at the

University of Iowa. What we learned at the university we also taught to the small kids at our church. This helped them get good exercise, get out of the streets, understand balance, and focus their mind. It seemed like we had something going on every single day. The good thing was that we would go as a family together and learn tae kwon do. It was quality family time.

The community was growing, and it was becoming the bedroom community of many University of Iowa employees in Iowa City. The growth and development of Iowa City seemed to move north and west, where our churches were located, North Liberty on the northwestern part and Tiffin on the western side. Leth became more active in the life of the church until one day she told me that she wanted to get into the ministry. She started an outreach ministry in the Coralville area at the trailer park community near Tiffin. She went to seminary at Dubuque University and started to take courses for another master's degree, Master of Ministry.

This was the year when we were so busy. We were all busy studying. I was working and finishing my doctoral studies at Saint Paul School of Theology, and Diwang and Amy were both in school and involved with many extracurricular activities. While Leth was working at the University as a nursing aide, volunteering at the church, and now taking some seminary courses, I was also contemplating the military chaplain ministry. Some of our church members were in the Iowa National Guard. These members gave me encouragement to explore this ministry.

Iowa City lost their US Army National Guard chaplain, and I was asked to explore this ministry. I had prayed once to do some chaplain work, and the opportunity came. I showed interest in this opportunity, and one day I got an offer from the recruitment office of the US Army Chaplain Corps, to which I responded affirmatively.

I submitted all the required documents for acceptance. All my education was very beneficial for my immediate acceptance. It was also timely that I had just finished my doctoral degree and was ready for another challenge. The bishop, and the Board of Higher Education and Division of Chaplain and Related Ministries endorsed my chaplaincy immediately. Upon acceptance, I was called to report to the Iowa Army National Guard (ARNG) in Iowa City. There I was commissioned as 1ˢᵗ Lieutenant of the US Army, and then sent to basic training for chaplaincy in the National Guard

My church endorsed my decision to be a National Guard reserve of the US Army. Since many of my church members were retired or had been in the military, and some were currently serving in the Iowa ARNG, they accommodated my extra work at weekend trainings. Since the church was also growing, we started to discuss the possibilities of asking for a solo-pastor for each church. I sensed that North Liberty United Methodist Church could be self-supporting, while Tiffin UMC could be attached to another small church. Or Tiffin UMC could receive assistance from the conference since it was in the church growth program. This proposal created controversies, but there were a few able leaders that worked together to pursue this dream.

As I got involved with the US Army National Guard, I started to enjoy this kind of ministry. It was not just the extra pay and the opportunity to minister to young soldiers that I enjoyed so much, but also the training the army provided all the chaplains. All these seemed very beneficial in my ministry. In our chaplains' seminar, they offered the possibility of active duty in a three-year commitment for all of us National Guard Reserve chaplains. We were told that after three years we could decide to make it as a career or quit if it was not the right calling of ministry.

I talked to Leth, who was then in the middle of her seminary schooling. I told her that we could try this ministry for three years, and if it was not the ministry we wanted to pursue, then we could come back into the parish church. I was persuasive and told her that it was just like receiving another appointment for three years except that this appointment would be beyond the state, because it could be in another state or in some other part of the world.

Leth seemed very adventurous, so I got her to agree that she would continue her seminary schooling until she finished. With Leth supporting me, it was lot easier for both of us to convince Amy and Diwang to try this new venture. At first I sensed their fear and reluctance, because their closest friends were there, but they also knew that they would eventually leave after a few years because of the system of appointment in place under the United Methodist Church. The process of acceptance to active duty was a lot easier since I was already in the Army National Guard Reserves. It was not long before I received the order for active duty.

My first tour of duty was Fort Polk, Louisiana. The army was so considerate that they allowed our kids to finish that school year (1990) before we went to Fort Polk. My colleagues in the National Guard made fun of me because they knew it would be harder work in active duty than in the National Guard. Furthermore, they thought that there was a better possibility of deployment to a real war than in the Guard. But they were proven wrong. When the Iraq conflict broke into war, the 109th Medical Battalion of Iowa City were called to war while my new unit in the active duty was supporting those who went to war. I thought I had the last laugh.

Chapter 8

Joining Uncle Sam

T he long-awaited month of June 1990 finally came. The Iowa Conference finally gave me the official appointment as chaplain of the US Army. The whole family was so excited to answer Uncle Sam's request to join the army. The move was more exciting because it was out of state and not a local parish, but rather an institutional setting—the Fort Polk US Army base in the state of Louisiana. We left North Liberty to go to the Iowa Conference, and from the conference we were on our way to Fort Polk, Louisiana.

It was a long drive, but there was enough time to see some scenic areas on our route. We stayed in Arkansas for one night and arrived in Fort Polk on the June 10. We stayed in the guesthouse of the base. The following day, I was assisted by a chaplain (CH) and chaplain assistant (CA). (CH is a clergy or commissioned officer; CA refers to a noncommissioned officer assisting a chaplain.) They helped me get acquainted with what to do and where to go. I had to report when I arrived on June 11, 1990, the day I was finally accepted as an active-duty chaplain. The assigned chaplain graciously assisted me until I got my order to serving as battalion chaplain. After all the processing, I finally got my official order to be chaplain of the First 5th (aka: 1/5) Field Artillery Battalion of Fort Polk, Louisiana.

I was promoted from 1st Lieutenant to captain of the US Army. My transition from reserve to active duty was fast. It was a thrilling experience because I gained lots of respect in my unit, not only as a chaplain but also as staff, an officer, and a religious adviser. My family's excitement in that first week began to disappear when we were still waiting for a place to stay. The hotel room was too small for the four of us even though the room was designed for a family of four. Leth tried to keep busy, making the kids play and go to the swimming pool every day.

Amy and Diwang started to gain new friends. Amy started to make me worry because she was getting some of the young soldiers' attention. I shared some of my anxieties with Leth, but she seemed more understanding than me. She said, "Let her enjoy the attention." By asking many questions about those who moved in, I finally understood that it would be better if we did not stay in a hotel but rather rent or buy our own house. After assessing my income and our possible expenses, I realized it was probably more feasible for us to buy a house than rent one.

The realtor took Leth and me to Leesville. We went to DeRidder to see more available housing. DeRidder had the best housing, but it was a little farther from Fort Polk, and my commute would be longer. We ended up taking a decent house in Leesville that was more affordable. The neighborhood was not that bad, and many people in the area were also soldiers. My family was so desperate to leave the military hotel, so buying a house was indeed a blessing. So, Leesville became our new home. It was our first owned house. We lived mostly in parsonages owned by the churches we served. Now we could call this house our own.

Within a week of entering the unit, the artillery brigade and the battalion were in the field having an intensive training in preparation to go to the desert of California, called the National Training Center (NTC) in Fort Erwin, California. I was busy training in preparation for the NTC. Within two weeks, I was on my way to the desert with the entire battalion. I didn't have a CA to work with me; however the unit gave me a staff sergeant as my driver, and he would serve temporarily as my CA. It was good to know I had my own driver and my own Humvee (a military vehicle often referred to as a Hummer). Unluckily, I didn't have a radio to communicate.

My family was so upset because I didn't have enough time to help them get settled in the new area, unlike in the parish ministry. The unit was in high-speed training. Since I was the only chaplain in the unit, I needed to catch up with their training and activities. Leth also had to transition from civilian to military life. I could not be with her, so she had to learn by herself how to survive in the military setting, and so did I.

I was to go to the NTC for a few weeks but was still unsure of what I was supposed to be doing. The brigade chaplain (CPT) Mackey briefed me on what to do and what to bring with me, but still everything was so new to me. Most of the time, I was lost. There were so many things to do, to prepare, and to bring. I started wondering if my family and I would ever survive in the military life. It was so different.

Deployment finally came. Whether we were ready or not, we were on our way to the NTC. Prior to my arrival, I heard so many negative comments about the place. CH (CPT) Mackey described the location as "a desolate, dry, sandy land that when God created the world, all His frustration went into creating the land in the NTC." We traveled by plane while our vehicles went ahead of us via train. We got to the NTC. The whole brigade gathered and built their individual tents, and the desert became like a tent city. As far as I was concerned, the environment looked pretty good. Perhaps because the experience was new to me, all I saw was a thrill and a new adventure. I knew I would learn a lot.

I began to realize that I would be preoccupied with lots of counseling. Every day, someone was referred to me. Some wanted to see the chaplain for almost any reason, such as domestic problems, drugs and alcohol, suicide attempts, getting out of the army, conscientious objector, divorce, financial problems, religious issues, etc. As I listened to all the soldiers' issues, I began to picture the kinds of ministries I would like.

After we gathered all our vehicles and equipment, we moved to the training field. The days never got boring for me. I got to do lots of the real-world soldier activities as well as participate in combat scenarios. The field was so dangerous. If we were not careful, we could be hurt or even die. I could easily get lost. The landscape all looked the same. At one time, we were heading to see another unit in my battalion. We were given the grid. I had studied this in my basic training, but I had forgotten exactly how to do it, so I had to depend on my chaplain assistant, Staff Sergeant (SSG) Briones, who according to the first sergeant (1SG) would be more dependable than a specialist (SPC). As we were heading north, we saw "live fire" (footnote: which are explosive shells which can create large land explosions and can be considered deadly) ahead of us. Suddenly an observing comptroller (OC) drove fast behind us screaming. They called off the training. Getting lost in the field nearly cost us our lives.

Later we found out that because of our stupidity, the training was called off. I was so angry with my chaplain assistant, who was supposed to know better. Since I was the officer, the responsibility was still mine. I was embarrassed when I saw my battalion commander, LTC Murphy. I thought he would scold me and give me disciplinary action. To my surprise, he just told the staff around him, "That is my chaplain, all right." Then he said to me, "Chaplain, you scared us when you were heading to the live fire."

What else could I say except "I'm sorry, sir, next time I will be more careful."

He made me feel better when he said, "Well, that is why we are here, to learn and do better."

After that experience, I took over the map. My chaplain assistant and I studied the map carefully. I discovered that if we got lost, it was easier to get back into the rear. The entire NTC was just like a very big circle, and there were certain places where the artillery units could be located. With that in mind, there was still some terrain that was hard to locate, because everything looked the same. So we still got lost. When I was not quite sure what I was doing, I asked. Amazingly, many of us were also learning, so I felt I was not alone. Perhaps the hardest part was the night operation when we were moving without light from midnight until dawn. We would just follow the convoy, but with the dust and rocks (some big rocks), it became difficult to stay with the convoy.

Sometimes we stayed too long on the road unmoved and in park. The temptation to snooze was so inviting. We were encouraged to get up and out of the vehicle and stretch out or walk around the vehicle. If the vehicle's driver in front of us accidentally went to sleep and the front started moving, the one left behind would be easily separated. This would create another group from the main group. The one left behind would eventually lead another group. If the one in front didn't know how to navigate, there would be another group lost in the desert. I knew this because I was part of that group, and sadly I was the one leading the group. Since I was the senior officer in that separated convoy, all the blame was on me.

If I had not been an officer, the soldiers would have probably cursed me. They probably did behind my back. Indeed, my chaplain assistant and I went to sleep. When we woke up, the vehicles ahead of us were gone. We looked around but found no vehicle moving except some chemical lights. I remembered we were once told that if we got lost, just follow the blue chemical lights. That's exactly what I told my chaplain assistant. At the end of the chemical lights, we found the aviation unit that was also using blue chemical lights.

We were really in trouble. The dawn light was already up and the sun started to shine. I accidentally found our battalion tactical operations center (TOC). From the TOC, I got the grid information where our headquarter unit was located. The battery commander was looking for us already, so we just needed to wait for him. The unit could not communicate because behind my convoy had the signal squad and the mechanics. I was so embarrassed for another mistake I had made. No one made a comment, but I knew my soldiers—they did it behind my back. I remembered we had several accidents that night, but thank God we did not have any deaths.

During our staff meeting, we briefed the commander about what happened that night in our convoy. It was reported that I got lost and led the convoy astray but found safety. The commander just looked at me, smiled, and said, "Our chaplain is learning." My fellow officers were laughing and kidding me. It might have been funny for them, but I knew it wasn't good for my record at the chaplain's OC. Well, what else could I do? It was done. I could do better next time. These were good learning experiences, but I learned the hard way.

The NTC was an experience I would never forget. It was an exciting experience at first, but it became boring because we did the same thing all over again. Then we went back to Fort Polk and had a few breaks. After that we went back to the field, trying to train for another NTC.

Each commander had to prove his ability to command and synchronize the battalion to work together as a team to win a war.

I stayed for three years with the 1/5 Field Artillery Battalion (FA Bn) and then was changed to 14th First (14/1) FA Battalion as the entire US military started downsizing. I went so many times to the NTC. I started hating the dust, the cold, and the hot weather. We almost lost one soldier to a flash flood during the rainy season. However, I always enjoyed being with my soldiers, seeing and visiting them, counseling them when needed. Perhaps this was what made me stay in the US Army. The ministry opportunities seemed unlimited. I was so busy both in the rear as well as in combat training. This was perhaps the most rewarding consolation I got from my daily military activities.

After a few months, the family moved. They too started to appreciate the military life. The kids had new friends. Both Amy and Diwang were doing well at school. Meanwhile, Leth was busy in her voluntary work at the main chapel as well as in the brigade chapel, where I was personally assigned. Also, Leth continued her seminary schooling until she finished her Master of Divinity degree at the University of Dubuque Theological Seminary in Iowa. After her schooling, she did not stop looking for a job until she got one. Luckily—or, I should say, in God's gracious favor—she found a United Methodist Church in DeRidder that was looking for a youth minister. She was hired quickly, and that kept her busy in addition to some of her volunteer work in the two chapels, in my unit, and with the Red Cross.

Amy revived her ballet skills that she learned in Iowa. She started teaching the small children at my unit some ballet moves. She choreographed an interpretative dance for the unit's Christmas program. Her voluntary involvement with the unit made her noticed by some of my young soldiers. I felt like she enjoyed all this attention. She also seemed to enjoy driving her car with my military sticker that showed the owner's officer rank. Every time she passed the gate, soldiers in attention gave a salute to the car she was driving. She was so thrilled to see good-looking young soldiers saluting her every time she passed the army's checkpoint. She probably thought they were saluting her, but I had to explain to her that it was the sticker on the car that required the courtesy of a military salute.

Diwang started to build up his own group of friends, a support group among the officers' kids, especially when we moved to the Fort Polk officers' housing area. We found out that we would save more money staying in the army base than staying elsewhere. It was also advantageous for Leth to drive to work in DeRidder and volunteer at the army chapels. Diwang joined the soccer and basketball teams for the military kids. Leth kept the whole family busy and took care of a lot of our kids' activities, especially when I was training either in the field or at the NTC. Amazingly, Leth quickly learned the ins and outs of the military system that she too had to help many military spouses, especially the newcomers. As a result, she received two awards, one from the artillery brigade (the "Molly Medal Awards") and one from the Fort Polk Garrison (the "Family Volunteer Achievement Awards").

Before the end of my third year, I received my order to go to Germany for my second tour of duty overseas. This was also the year for Amy to graduate high school and go to college. We traveled and checked several prospective universities where Amy would spend her higher education. Our home state offered a better deal, since we would no longer pay out-of-state school fees. Amy seemed to like the idea, because she had already many friends in Iowa. We also felt secure because our relatives and close friends were just a few hours' drive from the university.

Our Fort Polk experience was not all smooth sailing, but we also encountered some challenges that kept us growing. Amy had two car accidents during those years, and one of them ended up being very expensive. It scared us so much, and Amy had to learn to drive more carefully. It was also the reason that Leth decided to buy a new car before I left for Germany.

That was also the year when Amy started to be more rebellious, insisting on her independence like other teenagers. I also thought that Amy and Leth had more conflicts, perhaps because Leth was always with the kids. Amy was in love with a young soldier in my unit, but they broke up. Amy, in her young mind, thought that was the end of her life, and she almost ended her life. I was so scared when I picked up my daughter and took her to the hospital. Leth was at the University of Dubuque Theological Seminary when this occurred. I had so much guilt and many emotions. Thank God she just drank a handful of allergy pills. It could have been fatal or ruined her health for her entire life. I sensed God was still watching over us and caring for us.

The week when Amy had to leave for the university, she and her mom had another conflict. Amy said, "I can hardly wait to leave this house."

Leth was so hurt that she almost refused to deal with her anymore. But when she saw her packing, she still went to help her. I told Leth, "Amy is just like you, stubborn, and she wants things done her own way. You are alike. That is why you don't get along with each other."

"I just want her to be happy when she leaves home," Leth commented. After her separation from us, Amy was very happy with her new found independence. And the three of us—Diwang, Leth, and I—went overseas to my new tour of duty, Nuremberg, Germany. We were excited about this new assignment in June 1993.

Leth and Mel at Minorah Hospital 2nd day after Amy was born

Leth and Mel attending Leth sister's wedding.

Leth and Mel at St. Paul School of Theology, Kansas City, Missouri.

Leth and Diwang at Fort Polk, Louisiana.

Leth graduated the same year as Mel graduated.

Mel and Leth at North Liberty UMC.

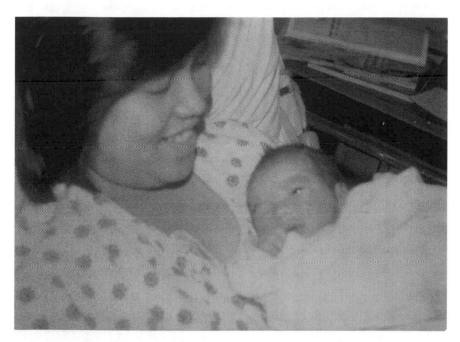

The day Diwang, our son, was born in Rock Valley, Iowa.

Family vacation at Rock City in Chatanooga, TN. (Leth, Diwang, Mel and Amy)

*Amy's baptism at Old Mission UMC. This picture
was taken in the church basement.*

*Diwang's baptism at Inwood, Iowa. Travis and Mary
Kathryn Wyatt visited our family.*

Amy, Diwang and Leth watching Mel playing his new musical toy.

Mel, Diwang, Leth and Amy during Christmas at Inwood, Iowa in 1980.

Mel and Leth in Bamberg, Germany in 1996.

Leth and Amy, bonding. Amy was three-years old.

Leth and Mel visited Korea in 1990.

The serious side of Aleta Valdez.

The family that studies together, stays together!

Mel's 50th Birthday at Harker Heights, Fort Hood, TX.

Chapter 9

The Europe Journey

We arrived in Frankfurt and then flew to Nuremberg, Germany, our final destination. We stayed at the downtown hotel where most military personnel stayed while in process. My new unit appointment was the 793rd Military Police Battalion. My sponsor was helpful in orienting me with the community as well as with the unit. It was our first time in Germany. When Amy was still a small kid, we went to some parts of Europe, but not Germany. We had plenty of time to get acquainted with the city, and the hotel was in downtown Nuremberg.

The city was beautiful. Downtown and the train station were within walking distance. I could tell Leth and Diwang would enjoy our new place. Diwang started to find some other kids from Fort Polk who moved also to Nuremberg. This was the location of the largest US military post exchange and commissary in Europe. So we enjoyed being able to shop for cheaper products, with more choices, that the military base offered. In addition to our private car, the public transportation in Europe was excellent.

After my documents were processed and I was oriented with my unit and garrison responsibilities, I began to see that my ministry would be lot different from the artillery unit. My areas of operation would be larger, covering sixteen campsites around the Bavaria communities of Germany. Our 793rd MP Battalion unit was mostly in charge of reinforcing the traffic, law, and order within the assigned campsite with occasional field training within the squad and/or subunits. We did the day to day supervision and ordering of the community, rather than the combat training. However, we also needed to do other types of trainings in order to maintain the skills of our soldiers. The entire battalion field training varied. We went to the field for field combat training and to urban camp training sites to house search, riot dispersals, civilian evacuations, etc. While some were training, we also needed some squads to cover the daily operation at each campsite (*kaserne*) within the sixteen communities. We found it so difficult to go as a whole battalion for training due to our daily responsibilities at the rear.

My battalion commander trusted my judgment and my program as long as I kept him informed of what was going on within the battalion, the soldiers' morale, and the soldiers' families. The commander and I were probably the most traveled personnel within the unit, because we were all dispersed in small groups throughout the Bavarian community. Since we covered some of the scenic and tourist spots of Germany, I also had the chance to enjoy taking my family to see these places. Once in a while, I used my field gear only when I decided to visit some squads or platoons that happened to be in the field. Every day I traveled with my chaplain assistant.

As the army continued to downsize, army *kasernes* were also decreasing. In a few months our operation went down to nine *kasernes*. And after a year of our stay, we were closing Nuremberg. Our battalion headquarters was to move to Bamberg. While we were in Nuremberg, Leth again volunteered in the chapel and with the Red Cross. On weekends we found the Volksmarch as a great way of spending family time. A day before weekend, we chose a Volksmarch event close to the community. Early in the morning we found the place, registered for a prize, and walked at least two miles. Then we claimed the memorabilia reward in the form of a beer glass or a mug. This was a fun way of exercising, getting in good family time, getting to see places, and getting to know people and understand the culture.

Leth also found a job, first at Nuremberg Army Elementary School as a part-time special education teacher, and then she found a full-time job as a preschool teacher at the army *kaserne* in Kitzingen, Germany. She commuted every day, but it did not last long, because our unit was to move to Bamberg. The *kaserne* in Nuremberg was in the process of closing. The commissary and the Post Exchange (aka: PX) would also close soon. Since our army unit base had the largest PX and commissary across Germany, there were so many products for sale at a much lower price than the original.

Leth really enjoyed buying things even though I didn't think we needed them. I just let her do it since she had her own job. I told her at times that whatever money she made she could enjoy spending. That was exactly what she did. She always purchased three items, saying, "One for us, one for Amy, and one for Diwang." She found out later that her taste was completely different from our kids. Our kids kept only a few things, and the rest of the things she bought she ended up giving away to relatives and friends. At least she enjoyed buying what she thought she would like.

Our unit was the last one to leave Nuremberg. We were responsible for closing the army base. We started moving personnel and families to Bamberg. We were packing again. Since we were close to Bamberg, the truck came to pack and load all our household goods that same day. At the end of the day, we were done and had the place ready for us at Bamberg. It was a long day of work, and we pulled out of the driveway with the truck. The truck supposedly would follow us because they didn't know the housing area where we were going.

As we yielded at the Autobahn, I could see them behind us, following us until we merged into heavy traffic in Erlangen. I tried to slow down in spite of the heavy traffic, but in those curves I lost the truck. When we reached outside the town and passed the heavy traffic, I tried to stay on the side with my flashing emergency lights, waiting for the truck to show up. But after thirty minutes of waiting, I decided to look for an exit in order to turn around. I didn't see the truck as I headed in the opposite direction. I turned around again at the last corner where I lost sight of the truck. I started getting nervous. I didn't know the license plate number of the truck and failed to get the full name of the driver and his assistant. We went to Bamberg and asked the gate soldiers if there was a truck that came in and they said, "Negative!"

I had to report this to the authorities, and they asked about the kind of vehicle, the plate number, and the name of the driver. I felt so embarrassed because I didn't know the vehicle's license plate number or the name of the driver. I remembered the kind of vehicle they used to haul my household goods. It was a Volvo, but of course that did not help much. If the driver took all our household goods, we would lose all we had worked for. Since it was just a day's move, we did not pay too much attention to signing all the necessary papers. This means we did not know the name of the company (since there were hundreds of contracting companies that the army hired to move soldiers) or any phone number to get ahold of someone who hauled our goods.

Leth and I were so restless and started to think of the worst-case scenario. Since I was a military police chaplain, our soldiers were kind enough to help me. They called the German police and started calling all the vehicle repair shops between Erlangen and Bamberg. We patiently waited in the empty house into which we were moving. We were hoping that someone would call us with good news. I could not sleep, so I drove again between Bamberg and Erlangen hoping to see the Volvo. It was midnight and I was really tired. Leth and Diwang were already asleep. I went to bed praying that the following day they would show up. Indeed, they did. When we woke up, the truck was outside the army base. The drivers were sleeping while waiting for us to wake up.

We were told their vehicle had broken down and they had to take the Volvo into a garage for repair. It was late at night when they were done, and they had to travel that same night to get to Bamberg. They wanted to call us, but we left no phone number and we too failed to get their company phone number. It was a good relief when I finally found them and they found us. This was a hard learning experience for us. The next move was that I was more careful than ever.

Bamberg was a beautiful city. Some claimed that it was the world capital of beer. All kinds of beers were in Bamberg, they claimed. I never checked if it was really true. All I could tell was that there were many beer companies in the area. Downtown Bamberg was as beautiful as Nuremberg. The nice thing was that there were bicycle routes going to downtown and the river walk. We bought a tandem bicycle since Leth didn't know how to bike. Diwang had his own bike, and we spent lots of time biking in the area whenever we could. It was great to spend quality family time in addition to the Volksmarch.

While in Bamberg, Leth found another good job in Wurzburg, supervising and certifying home child care providers for the US Army. She commuted an hour every day, but she seemed to enjoy her job. She traveled and visited houses of all those registered child care providers. She helped them implement the requirements of the army for quality care and renewal of the provider licenses to continue their operations. She liked her job working in and out of the office. The variation of her work kept her day interesting and short. At night, at least she was home with Diwang, especially when I was out or in the field.

Diwang's buddies kept him busy. He also continued to refine his art. One time I came home and found a stranger in my house opening the refrigerator. I asked the young man, "Who are you?"

He just looked at me without caution and replied, "Who are you?"

I said, "I am the owner of this house."

He just shrugged his shoulders and said, "Oh, I am Diwang's friend. I am just looking for a drink."

"Where is my son, then?" I asked.

I was a little bit offended because he didn't even look at me, and he continued to browse my refrigerator while talking. "Diwang is in his room taking a nap."

Later I found out that Diwang was doing the same thing at his friends' houses. So it was no longer a surprise that our food and drinks in the refrigerator didn't last too long. We had a squad that my son entertained every day. Leth thought it would be better if they came to our house to hang out rather than going to places that we didn't know and possibly getting into trouble. Sometimes they got rowdy, but Leth seemed to enjoy their company. She really loved hanging out with young people.

Meanwhile, our unit was getting ready for lots of training in preparation for deployment to Bosnia. I spent many days in the field with our soldiers in trainings, meetings, and chaplains' training within the brigade, the division, and the V Corps chaplains. These trainings and transitions were so stressful among us, especially the soldiers with families who just arrived to the unit and did not expect to be deployed that soon. I did a lot of counseling during this period in the unit because of suicides or attempted suicides, domestic violence, a conscientious objector, divorce threats, single female soldiers trying to get pregnant prior to the deployment, and other soldiers trying to get out of the army for other reasons.

Amazingly, the day came and we were ready to roll. Families showed their support for us as we left our base unit. To some it was a very emotional departure, and the support was well expressed by the friends and families waving their American flags to us. It was very early in the morning, and it was still dark and very cold. I saw my family waving their flags while Leth was hiding her face to keep her warm from the cold wind.

As usual, the hurry-and-wait military tradition was still alive, even in deployment. We reached Frankfurt, Germany, early in the morning at the air force base, and we lined up among the other battalions who were already waiting for liftoff. It took us several days before we left the base because of some regulations to satisfy the air force requirement of deployment. In addition to all these regulations, there were icy conditions so that we had to turn around in Hungary and return. Spouses, including my wife, took special trips to Frankfurt just to come and see us prior to our flight. We slept on the floor at the airport but ate decent meals at the mess hall or at the fast-food restaurant.

Early in the morning we were called to get ready and told that the Hungary airport field was now clear for our safe landing. For the second time, we were on our way. In front of me was my Humvee. It was great because I had a vehicle to use right away when we arrived at our destination. We arrived in Hungary with almost zero visibility. We barely saw the guiding lights and the people working in the area; however, we managed to land safely.

Chapter 10

Deployment for Peace

Hungary was snowing the day we arrived. The roads were muddy. The soldiers in our unit, who were ahead of us, prepared the shelter for us. We arrived in the area on January 1, 1996. The New Year's celebration dinner was steak to help upgrade the soldiers' morale. There were clean, warm showers and nice bathrooms. We heard so many horrible stories about what was happening in Hungary, but it was not bad at all. The mess hall was large enough to hang around in. The phones to call home were a few meters from the mess hall. Some units also had available phone lines. My unit set aside a place for me to do my counseling, if needed.

In spite of the busy schedule, we had the chance to get out of the base and see the town. CH (LTC) David Campbell, our brigade chaplain, took us to different places inside and outside the base. Our 2nd MP Brigade Unit Ministry Team got closer as we worked together and planned for our ministries when we got to Tuzla, Bosnia. It was great to work with the brigade, because we always received updated news about what was going on around the entire division and why we had so many delays. The 709 MP Bn went ahead of us and encountered the first mine accident. The good Lord was watching over them in spite of the accident, and no one was killed or seriously injured.

The bridge that connects Croatia and Bosnia was destroyed. The engineering unit created a temporary floating bridge to allow units to cross the river. Meanwhile, our soldiers stayed for a week or more in Hungary waiting for the order to move. Many of them were getting restless. No one could get settled. We packed and got ready every day, but we waited for nothing. The hurry-and-wait motto! When we were told it was ready for real movement, almost no one believed and shrugged their shoulders. But that late afternoon call was the marching order. We lined up according to the movement in which we were trained. We were informed that once we reached Bosnia, no one was allowed to leave the perimeter of the vehicles or the route because of the possible mine explosions.

We were given a urinal plastic container in case we needed it. Senior officers were instructed on how to give women space and support their hygiene. Our vehicle was loaded with not only our personal belongings and our UMT military gear, but also some soldiers' gear that didn't fit in the other vehicles. We left Hungary late in the afternoon and entered the Croatia expressway when it was almost dark. We stopped at the rest area, and to our surprise we were asked to pay for using the restrooms with Croatian money. Some of us left and used the corner walls. Finally, the owner allowed us to use the bathroom, especially our female soldiers who needed it badly. We tried to pay them in our dollars, and they graciously accepted it.

As we got closer to the border, we moved slowly without our headlights and we were all on alert. Since it was so dark, we could not tell where we were. We were told to go ahead and sleep, except one person in each vehicle had to stay awake. It was very cold, so we left our Humvee running to keep us warm. I let my assistant go to sleep first, and we took turns. As the dawn came and the sun started to rise, we found that we were already in line with the other units that were ahead of us. We were already in the vicinity of the river and waiting for our turn to cross.

It took almost all day before we were able to cross the river. The crossing was done very slowly. The floating bridge was well managed by the military engineers with two boats keeping the bridge still in spite of the strong current of the large river. I never heard about any accident while crossing the river, so it must have been done professionally. As we entered Bosnia, I was surprised at how welcomed we were by the nationals. Children and adults were waving their hands, a gesture of welcome. I heard some saying "Bravo!" and "Welcome!" and "Clinton is a good man!" I was expecting more resistance, as we always heard from the media, but we did not.

In spite of those wonderful gestures, we stayed alert and watchful. We passed through different communities and saw on our way so many destroyed and burned houses. There were some communities where houses were totally destroyed. What seemed strange was that between the destroyed houses there were houses that were not touched at all. Later on we found out that the destroyed houses were owned by the Muslim Bosnians, and the untouched houses were owned by the Christian Bosnians. It was so unbelievable how these two parties hated each other for whatever irrational reason.

The movement that night was a long journey. It was snowing and the road was dangerous. Some of our vehicles had a few accidents, but no one was injured. We arrived at our destination, Tuzla West, at dawn. It was still dark and no one was allowed to leave the vehicle until it was cleared or free from mines. Those who wanted to stretch out could do it only either behind or in front of their vehicles. As the sun rose up, we saw many children already playing and watching us. Some thought they could get out since the kids were already playing around, but the order was strict.

Kids were getting closer to us, asking for food and for almost anything they could get from us. One soldier was about to throw a plastic bag full of human waste and warned the kids, "This is not for you. It is poop! It smells bad!" The young soldier thought he made himself clear, but the kids did not understand the language. He threw the plastic bag as far as he could, and the kids ran after it. The young soldier was screaming not to touch it. The first kid who took the plastic bag after opening it screamed and cursed while the rest of the kids laughed at him. It was a bad experience for both parties.

Because of the number of kids roaming around in our area, the commander finally declared that the area was clear and safe. We started to choose the areas where we could build our tent. My chaplain assistant found a place where we could be easily accessible when the soldiers needed us. It did not last long. Our group started to grow as different units from our brigade arrived. When I started counseling more, the commander gave me a hex tent to build. We built the tent away from the busy area to preserve some soldiers' privacy. I built my own table and bench out of the shipping lumber used to box some fragile army equipment.

Any scrap lumber became a treasure. We gathered it to build furniture and a stepping bridge to connect one tent to another and avoid stepping on mud. Occasionally, my Bn Commander LTC Knoblock came to see me and checked on the morale of our soldiers. He also asked my morale and how he could be more helpful to me. It was a good feeling to see a commander interested in my personal and professional welfare.

The aviation brigade arrived and occupied the other side of the camp. As we continued to grow, the area also continued to develop until the camp was comfortable to live in. It became like a little city, with a PX store, a theater, a chapel, warm water for showers, restrooms, phone booths, a barbershop, laundry rooms, a gym for physical fitness, electricity to keep soldiers' personal radios and televisions on, a large mess hall, fast food, etc. All these were built in tents. Our quarters had central air and heaters. Twice a day—and, if we were lucky enough, three times a day—we had warm meals. We had many local nationals who cooked our food and sometimes served us their local bread and pastries.

In addition to having Bible study and worship, I sponsored a language class. I invited a Bosnian interpreter, Alma, to teach our soldiers some basic language tools in order to communicate with the nationals. Since our battalion was widely dispersed, I had the chance to see many camps across Bosnia and Serbia. I also saw human corpses untouched on the road in some isolated areas. One of our platoons that was assigned outside Bosnia occupied a very scenic area that used to be the Muslim village located in Serbia. All of the houses in this mountainous area were completely destroyed. You could see some blood stains on the walls and pictures scattered.

Outside the village was a city where most of the Serbians lived. Most houses were intact except the few that were destroyed. It was obvious that the destroyed houses in that neighborhood were owned by the Muslims. Every move was made with caution. I moved to visit our soldiers dispersed in different camps only when there was an available convoy moving to that area. Sometimes when I was needed, a convoy came to fetch me. When the high-ranking rabbis came to visit the Jewish soldiers, our brigade UMTs sponsored them. We took them to visit some of our Jewish soldiers who were spread throughout the country. We flew by helicopter, which was my first time flying in a military helicopter.

We also helped the rabbis prepare their food for their Passover celebration. It was a very unique experience to see how they actually prepared the food and the way they celebrated this important Judeo-Christian festivity. The soldiers got so rowdy at the end of the event that I presumed they were drunk. After the festivity when everybody left the area, we heard that some soldiers got into trouble and were arrested. Alcoholic beverages were strictly prohibited in the IFOR operation, but the group was allowed to drink because it was a part of their religious ceremony. The arrest of those soldiers who came from the festivity created embarrassment for the rabbis.

Our chapel had so many activities and was busy day and night. We had to have personnel on twenty-four–hour duty. Since we had two brigades, we took turns according to our availability. Chaplains did the same. But we had the freedom to move around and visit our units dispersed across the country. There were so many small units attached to us that we needed to provide coverage. Even though we had our own chapel, we retained a hex tent to serve as my personal office, study, place of spiritual prayer and devotion, and a place of private counseling for my own soldiers. It was good for me to keep my day short and busy.

During Lenten season, we received so many letters, cards, cookies, candies, etc., from many people across the States reminding us that they were praying and supporting what we were doing. We even received clothing and many goods to distribute to the Bosnian nationals, especially to children. Unfortunately, we had to refuse this because we had no means to carry out this mission. Soldiers were even warned not to give food or leftovers from the Meal, Ready-to-Eat (MRE) because of previous experiences that almost endangered the life and mission of our soldiers.

Many kids would hang out near the soldiers because it meant food for them. Some of our soldiers were so generous that they gave some of their food out of the MREs. Each MRE bag had so many items that some soldiers could not eat all of it. They put any leftovers in a box and handed it to the kids. Sometimes the soldiers threw it to them when their vehicles were running. So, whenever kids saw soldiers, they started asking for food, and sometimes they started running after a convoy. A kid was almost run over because of this.

Also, some soldiers did not have enough to give, and those who did not receive anything started throwing stones at soldiers' moving vehicles. Some kids looking for food took the soldiers' duffel bags. One soldier who did not eat his MRE gave it to an adult. This spread out quickly, and groups of adults started asking for bags of MREs. They started making trouble for those who had nothing to give. All these experiences added up and endangered our soldiers' lives and mission.

Furthermore, many commanders felt that any mistake we did could create national media exposure that the enemies were itching to hear about. So they made a policy to stop giving out food, and anyone caught giving it out would be prosecuted. Some soldiers were so upset about it, especially those who did not understand the reason behind the policy. We were convinced that this policy could keep us from harming our mission and keep our soldiers safe.

In our camp, we tried to explain how this policy came about. We decided to make an alternative plan. We put a big box in the chapel for the leftover MREs, which would be distributed to the organized welfare agencies that deal with this kind of mission and could distribute the food appropriately. At the same time, we also tried to encourage the churches in the States to channel their giving through private welfare agencies or institutions because we were not manned to carry out this kind of mission.

Easter Sunrise was well planned, and each chaplain had specific responsibilities. I was to give the opening prayer for the Sunrise service. I was prepared. That Sunday I woke up early and took a quick shower. As

I went to the shower tent, I saw many soldiers heading in one direction. After the shower, I saw no one outside, and I started wondering if there was something going on that I didn't know about. I went to see my chaplain assistant, and he was not in bed. Suddenly he showed up and said, "Sir, what happened? They were waiting for you."

"Waiting for what?" I asked.

"For the Easter Sunrise!" he replied.

"Why? It's an hour early."

He said, "Sir, you did not adjust your time for daylight savings?"

I realized then that I had done something wrong. I rushed to the Sunrise service location, and the worship service was observed. My brigade chaplain, LTC David Campbell, knew then I had forgotten to adjust my time, and all I could do was apologize. Someone took my part, the opening prayer, when they could not find me. It was very embarrassing. But what could I do except accept my shortcoming. Hopefully, it would never happen again. I was feeling very uncomfortable, and it became worse when I was the center of teasing from my colleagues. I just shrugged my shoulder, smiled, and moved on.

Meanwhile, my order to go to school had already arrived. My replacement was also on his way to Bosnia. I informed Leth about when I would leave the theater to go to Bamberg and when we had to leave to go back to the States. My new tour of duty was back in Fort Polk, Louisiana. Fort Polk had become the home of the Joint Readiness Training Center (JRTC), a training center for the US Army. The time was getting too short. Leth alone had to plan on how to ship our household goods and at the same time keep her job in Wurtzburg.

The first shipment would be any items that were necessary for setting up our new home in Louisiana. This would include basic household items like clothing, towels, cooking utensils, etc. The second shipment would include large household items like furniture, appliances, etc. The second shipment included our first vehicle. The last shipment would be the basic supplies we had been using while everything else was shipped. Most of these supplies would actually travel via plane with us to our new home. It was a lot of work for anyone to handle alone.

While I was waiting for the last day of my Bosnia tour, Leth was calling me almost every day and begging for me to come home early because she could not handle all the pressure of moving alone. This was her first time moving without me. There were times she called me crying. She felt as if the movers didn't listen to her or respect her. They seemed to be Turkish and she felt belittled by their attitudes and behaviors. She said they would not listen to her the way they listened to men.

In Bosnia, my team was busy planning for my going-away party, while I too was busy clearing out the theater. My CA acted strangely unsupportive since I was done with his evaluation report; perhaps he was ready for a new guy to be his boss. My commander, the staff, and some of my soldiers were very appreciative to my ministry, especially those I had helped in counseling. I left West Bosnia early in the morning with the help of the brigade CA. After briefing, we rode the bus across Bosnia with our Kevlar, and when we reached Croatia, we removed all our gear and enjoyed the ride to Hungary.

The camp seemed quiet except for those who were being processed back into the military camps and those being processed out of the base. But it was a good feeling to be there, because there was nothing to fear and we could wear our light PT clothing. After out-processing, we had some fast food and were ready to move out again for a long ride, but this time we were heading home. We slept in the bus while moving, and by morning we were entering Germany. We reached our destination at Ram Mainz air force base to be in-processed again. It was so nice to see my wife waiting for me. Diwang was not with her. She had planned it that way so that we could be together and spend time with each other.

Leth had reserved a place in Frankfurt at a US Army officers' quarters for us to stay overnight. It was a very romantic night for us. We walked around Frankfurt, saw places, and relaxed in nice quarters. It was an exhausting night but a very good one for both of us. We overslept that night and then drove home. I was excited to see Diwang, but unfortunately he was not home. He was with his friends as always. Our apartment was already bare. Leth had already started painting the walls in preparation of turning it over to the base for inspection. In a few days, I had to move to Fort Polk so that I could be in-processed and ready to go to advance chaplain schooling. Leth agreed to stay behind to finish her work commitment with the Department of Defense (DoD) while I would go ahead to Louisiana to prepare our new home prior to leaving for military school.

Chapter 11

Military Schooling and JRTC

I was on my way to the States, and I stopped to see Amy, who happened to be in Iowa before heading back to Fort Polk. Meanwhile, Diwang stayed with his friends. Since our vehicle was not available yet, we had to borrow Amy's car to get by. I went straight to Fort Polk to report for duty. I started the process for transitioning back to Fort Polk and also claimed back our old house from the rental agency. In a few days we got notice that our BMW had arrived and I had to get it in New Orleans at the naval base. Our basic household goods had also arrived.

The chaplain assigned to assist me in my transition was very helpful. I was assigned to the garrison with three responsibilities. My main job was as mobilization chaplain for the reserve units of the garrison. The second, which ultimately became my main responsibility, was as the post chaplain of the gospel service. The third was covering one battalion that had no chaplain: the 509th INF Airborne Battalion Opposition Force (OPFOR).

Since I was en route to the advanced school for chaplains, I had no chance to get to know my new assignment. Leth was in Germany, Diwang was in Iowa, and I was in Fort Polk, Louisiana, getting busy to prepare the house before Leth arrived. The household goods arrived on time. I had the chance to unpack and arrange everything to make the house presentable and livable. Leth arrived a few days before I left Fort Polk for school. She was so delighted to see our place and all our things in place, except for a few boxes that were still untouched.

I had to rent a vehicle to go to Fort Jackson, South Carolina, for the chaplain's school so that Leth would have a vehicle to use. Our second vehicle (a GM Astro van) came at a later date. Diwang joined Leth because his school was about to start. In spite of all the preparation I had done, Leth had a lot more to do. When our second vehicle arrived by ship at the port, Leth had to take a bus to Texas in order to pick up the car. She arrived there at night because she had trouble locating the place. She told me she was scared because the place was so isolated and she had to walk a distance to get there. At least she arrived home safely, despite the long night drive.

My schooling took more than a month, including at least two weekends. Leth came to visit me at the school. I had to reserve a room in a hotel for her so that we could have our privacy. With all our separation since I had gone to Bosnia, then with our move from Germany, and now with my schooling, I really missed her. We had quality time together, like we were in another stage of our honeymoon. The weekends were great, but after that we were back again in the schoolroom.

School was not that easy. We had so many projects and requirements, including intensive physical exercises. Those who failed the physical fitness test were sent home. The last exam was a written test that took lots of my time reviewing for, as I feared getting a failed report to my commander. That would end my military career. The test was not easy, but I was happy I made it. Only a few students did not make it. My graduation day was a big sigh of relief. I was proud of another achievement. Leth came to my graduation, and we both drove home together.

The garrison chaplain had already briefed me about my threefold chaplain's duties. Though my main title would be reserve mobilization chaplain, my main responsibility would be as the administrative chaplain of the Gospel Congregation for the entire post. This was the largest protestant congregation in the entire post and the highest contributor to the chaplain's fund. My third responsibility was to be the unit chaplain of the 509th Airborne Infantry Battalion (Opposition Force or OPFOR). This battalion did not have a chaplain of its own.

The previous commander of the 509th Airborne at one time, I was told, did not see the need for a chaplain officer in his unit, so the army removed the chaplain. So for a long time they existed as a unit without their own chaplain. The battalion commander and his predecessors realized that they needed a chaplain. Now they had to request getting back their own battalion chaplain. Since the process of requesting a chaplain for a unit did not come that easy, I had to cover them in the garrison. This was a special force that trained many US Army units around the world, including foreigners and allies who came to Fort Polk.

With my three hats, I knew this would be a good experience, but at the same time I too would be spread thin. The experiences were never boring, and I enjoyed my job in spite of my busy schedule. Perhaps the most demanding was the administrative operation of the gospel service every Sunday. This was a protestant service highly attended by the black community of the military servicemen and their families, including retirees. This congregation was a delight to work with. They were organized, well dressed, and loving people. We had between five and ten volunteer lay preachers and several deacons. They were respectful of the clergies, and I enjoyed the way they treated my family and me.

The style of worship was far from the traditional experience I grew up with: the long service, the repetitious lyrics, the dancing and clapping and raising of hands, the wailing, and the fainting sometimes while praying. At one time I felt awkward clapping and dancing with the gospel music. However, as I grew with them, my son noticed that I started swinging my body while singing even when I was not with the gospel service. My son made fun of me, because he said my clapping was sometimes out of rhythm. Since no one cared, I just did it in the spirit of worship.

Another thing I liked about this group (though it was too conservative for me theologically) was that they took their faith very seriously. Almost half the congregation regularly attended a prayer group and Bible study every Wednesday. And at every gathering there was food to eat. Most members were noncommissioned officers (only one or two were commissioned officers), and most of them were among the lowest-ranking soldiers and their families. This meant that most members were not in a high-salaried bracket. But since many of these members took their faith and giving seriously, the gospel service congregations were the highest financial contributors of the entire post.

Their musicians were impressive. Even though very few could read music, the organist and pianist played without looking at any sheet music. Their drummers (one of whom was just a boy) played well. The preaching was mostly traditional. In response to the preaching, some members would say, "Amen!" or "Right on!" or "You got that right!" or "Give me more!" or "Preach on!" or "Hallelujah!" or "I am tracking!" or "Oh, yeah!" Since everyone was eager to preach, I had to schedule all those who claimed to be commissioned and ordained preachers of their denominations. All those who wanted to preach were required to have at least an endorsement certificate from their denomination.

Their cooperation made my job a lot easier since I was the chaplain accountable to the US Army for the entire operation of this congregation. I mostly coached all the leaders and volunteer workers, did administrative works, put together the programs and budget according to the SOP of the US Army, and made requisitions of the chaplain's fund to support our programs and activities. Since I served as their pastor of the Gospel Congregation, most of the soldiers and their families came to see me instead of their unit chaplains.

I kept busy every day at the office. Counseling was the dominant service I provided to the soldiers and their families, not only in my congregation but also to the 509th Airborne Infantry Battalion. The 509th Airborne INF (OPFOR) almost never deployed out of Fort Polk. However, almost every month they remained in the field to train soldiers who came to JRTC. When the unit was not that busy in the field, they jumped for their training. Since this unit was always in the field and in constant movement, their mission was also hard for their families, especially for the young soldiers with families and small kids.

I developed retreat/seminar combination geared toward young couples. I put together a marriage enrichment retreat, marriage encounter, and "True Colors" (a personal inventory seminar and workshop for success). My wife, Leth, arranged all the brochures and worksheets we had gathered for several years as a marriage enrichment training workshop (METW). As Leth and I continued to attend several leadership trainings on marriage enrichment, we picked up great ideas and put them together to make our METW. It was interesting and fun. We combined some play, workshop, poetry, dialogue, lectures, singing, testimonies, and Bible studies.

We emphasized that this METW was designed for leadership training in each unit at the battalion level in order to be helpful to the young families that were struggling in their relationships. Those who attended first spread the news that it was helpful, not only for them as leaders, but for their spousal relationships. Since the members of the first group were officers, the program became so popular that it became a monthly training. We started in a hotel until we found a new and beautiful conference facility in Alexandria, Louisiana, designed for small and large groups with food and lodging. The program was designed for the 509th INF Airborne BN. It became so popular that other units attended.

I owed the success of this program to Leth. She typed and helped me print all the materials we needed. She organized our schedules and almost all necessary details of the entire program. We even got her friend who was my battalion XO (aka: Executive Officer) to attend the program, and she liked it. Prior to the day of our METW, we would sit down and discuss how we would present the program in the most interesting way. Leth's involvement and input was deeply appreciated by the women who were in the METW. She was a real blessing and put in lots of time as well as money to make this program possible. The program was also introduced to the religious groups with some changes to fit the need of the religious community.

Of all the programs we did together, I considered this program a success due to the full support of my commander. Since it became a training seminar for our leaders, getting financial support from our S-4 (Logistics) became easier. The chaplain's fund also helped pay for some of our food and refreshments. As we continued to run this program, Leth and I found that it was helping both of us in our relationship. It was also helping our relationship with our kids. Furthermore, Leth told me how meaningful this training was for her, because some of the women in attendance personally thanked her for saving their marriages with the seminar. This was the kind of seminar that made us work together, not only as a couple, but as professionals. She became a great critique, mentor, teacher, colleague, and partner.

Our time in Fort Polk was great, but it was also a busy time for Leth and me. It was during this time that Leth got another pastorate job. She had been longing to have one. She had served as youth minister and associate pastor in the United Methodist Church in DeRidder, Louisiana, during our first tour in Fort Polk. During our second tour in Fort Polk, she became the administrative pastor serving a two churches of The United Methodist Church in Kinder, Louisiana. She liked the ministry and was always excited to tell me how her congregation was slowly growing in Sunday service attendance. Unfortunately, she had to be in Kinder while I was in Fort Polk. Her church provided her a parsonage where she could stay while Diwang and I stayed in Leesville, where we had our own house.

Since I loved to go fishing in the Gulf of Mexico, every Friday night on my way to fishing, I would pass by her parsonage, which was only fifteen or twenty more miles south. Fishing became the most therapeutic activity I had developed for my stressful life. The separation, my busy unit schedule, and the congregation I was serving were so stressful. I also had to finish my military schooling through correspondence in preparation for me to go to Fort Leavenworth, Kansas. This schooling was a prerequisite for a promotion to major of the US Army. When the time came to go to Fort Leavenworth, I thought Leth's church appointment was a blessing, because we would be separated but at least she would be busy. But that did not work well, because she too was worried about leaving our teenage son alone at home.

While I was at military school, I missed my family and started growing concerned about my son at home and Leth at her church. Leth managed to go home almost every night after work just to be with him. Sometimes she would take Diwang to her job, but that did not help much because Diwang had extracurricular school activities. I learned that the church told Leth that they needed a pastor who could stay in the parsonage so that when members needed her she would be accessible.

She took this to heart and continued to express her support for me so that I would not be distracted from my schoolwork.

School was extremely hard for me because of all the combat theories and war game operations. This was far from my ministry, but it was necessary for me to understand if I was to be in the military community. I noticed that I was not alone struggling with this study. There were also staff and officers who, like me, felt inadequate. It was comforting when our professor told us that most chaplains, lawyers, nurses, and doctors had the same trouble understanding the war game strategies and operations in combat. But it was vital that we understood these so that we knew how the total military worked and could provide the necessary services to our soldiers. In spite of the struggle, we had to work as a team, and those of us whose lives were in direct combat were willing to help us understand the total operation.

School was extreme, both academically and physically. We had to pass all these tests because our future depended on whether we could keep our military career. That was what I intended. It was a great relief when I passed the written exam. The second test was physical. I trained every day, but when the day came, it was one that I never expected. At dawn, I was already at the formation line for the army physical fitness test (APFT). I was ready. I had been doing great in the past, so I was confident I would make it. However, I wanted to excel and get the highest score possible.

I was probably the oldest in the class. Since I was the highest in rank, they made me their class executive officer (XO). I was surrounded by young officers,who were tall and strong. However, I was confident that I could beat some of them in running, push-ups, and sit-ups. The physical fitness test finally came. I started, and my push-ups and sit-ups were excellent, I was told. I felt so good and started stretching as we prepared for a two-mile run. I had a good start and saw that there were three of us ahead of everyone else. At about one and a half miles, I suddenly felt weak, and no matter how I exerted myself, I could not speed up. I felt like I could not reach the finish line. The worst thing was that one of my shoelaces was untied and it was dangling on my other foot.

Some members of my team started to pass me. I was gasping for air and feeling like I wanted to give up. Suddenly, I heard a voice saying, "Come on, Mel! A few more steps and you're done." I felt very weak, but I made it to the finish line. I saw my car and leaned on the hood to rest. Our leader was screaming at me not to stop but to keep walking. I could not walk, so someone helped me. Finally, I started to gain some strength and tried to walk, but I still felt weak.

On the way to my quarters, I could not talk very well. I just felt weak. My partner asked me several times if I was all right. I said I was okay except that I felt weak, like there was something heavy sitting on my chest. I told him to take me to my room, because all I needed was a little rest and I would be good. I reached my room and crashed on my bed but forgot to close my door. I was just resting before I took my shower. When my friend saw me, he said, "You don't look good, Mel. Whether you like it or not, I will take you to the clinic and then let them decide if you are okay."

He took me to the clinic, and my friend told them what happened. A nurse came to attend to me, and after checking my blood pressure, etc., she suddenly started telling doctors that I had a heart attack. They put me in the hospital bed, and quickly I was attended by several doctors and medical staff. I was so weak and sleepy, but they kept waking me up. I was taken by ambulance to the veteran hospital, where I was confined for several days.

After a night's stay, I was surprised when my wife arrived early in the morning. My military unit arranged to help my wife fly to be with me. That day, I had several lab tests, X-rays, etc. Then they took me to Kansas University Hospital in Kansas City. I was confined for two or three days. The test results reported that surgery was inevitable. I was asked to move to Walter Reed in Washington DC to do the surgery, but I was told it could be dangerous if we waited any longer. My wife and I made the decision to go ahead and do it all at the university hospital.

I was amazed to find out how quickly the news spread. Some old friends who lived in Kansas came to see me. I got lots of letters and calls from relatives and friends who were praying for me. My supervising chaplain also came from Fort Polk to see me and prayed for me prior to my surgery. It was Friday, and my doctor came to see me and asked if I wanted to go home first, prior to the surgery, which was scheduled for early Monday morning. I thought it would be a great idea to have a quick break prior to the surgery and to be with my wife without any interference from those nurses who came to check on me almost every hour.

The doctor seemed suspicious when he found out that I had been away from my wife for almost three months, so he made me sign a contract that I would not have sex if I went home. I thought that was ridiculous, but I signed it anyway. The doctor said, "I will let you go, but you two should behave."

I said, "No problem, Doc." It was a great feeling when I was temporarily released from the hospital, knowing I had a break before my big day.

We headed to my quarters, and my wife served me good food and a drink. We talked a lot, but then we passionately started hugging and kissing. Both of us were turned on by our strong desire and affection for each other. Leth pushed me and said, "Let us not do this. We made a contract and it could danger your health."

My desire was already out of control, and I told her, "I would rather die knowing I was with you than die in the surgery room regretting the happiness I received from you." Since I was determined and out of control, she convinced me to stay passive and she did everything until we both reached our climax.

She looked at me with concern and said, "How do you feel?"

I said, "Honey, I feel so great. But I also feel so weak and seem to be running out of breath, so don't talk to me for a while. I was a little worried because of the very strange feeling I had. I thought I would die that night and, if I did, I would have died happily."

She looked at me again with concern, but I was smiling at her. She said, "This is very stupid of us."

"Yes," I agreed, but it was good stupidity as far as I was concerned. "I am telling you I feel like I just came from heaven."

Both of us just laughed and hugged each other. She asked me, "What would I tell the doctor if you happened to die at the time of our lovemaking?"

"That would be your problem, not mine. Oh, just tell him I died very happy!" was my reply. As she always did, she scolded me.

On Sunday evening we went back to the hospital in preparation for my early bypass surgery. The doctor asked us, "Did you behave?"

We did not say anything but looked at each other and smiled. I asked the doctor instead, "Who will cut me, you or the old guy? Doc, what is my chance of survival?"

His wise answer was typical of many doctors: "We have done lots of successful surgeries here even though we say there is no guarantee. Most of my patients come out all right."

"Out of one hundred patients, what percentage have not made it?" I asked.

He said, "Let's not talk about that. Let's talk about you and what we will be doing for you."

That night, I slept well in spite of several interruptions by the nurses. Was I worried if I would die? Believe me, it was not my concern. I felt at peace with God. I even prayed to God that I might see him face-to-face the next day or after the surgery. I thought that those who came to see me were more concerned than I was. I knew I was ready for any circumstance. This was the essence of what I had been preaching, that there was "no fear" for those who loved the Lord.

The day finally came. Many doctors and medical staff came to brief me, and shortly I was on my way to the operating room. They put me to sleep. I was in a very deep sleep and could not remember anything except that when I woke up, I felt very cold and I heard voices asking my name and if I knew what day it was. I tried to respond, but I could not say anything except that I was freezing and felt no pain. They gave me warm blankets and I started feeling better. I didn't even know that the surgery was over until I became completely conscious. My wife stayed with me while some of the people who accompanied Leth were only allowed to see me from the window. Relatives and friends on both sides were with my wife, showing their support and care for us. Amy and Richard traveled from Arizona all night, crossing a snowstorm, just to see me.

My recovery was slow and painful. The military school allowed me to finish and graduate because my surgery occurred at the end of the semester. I had met all the requirements and passed the test prior to my surgery. Unbelievably, the school gave me a physical fitness award because I had a higher score in our group PT (aka: physical test). The chaplains and units I served were very supportive. Leth had to quit her pastorate work at the parish so that she could give me quality care for my immediate recovery. She did all she could to give me all that I needed for my immediate recovery. Fort Sam Houston, San Antonio, was the closest military hospital in Texas. We had to drive many miles for my routine health checkup. Leth pampered me with her loving and tender care.

Slowly, I got back to my normal routine. With the physical and occupational therapist's help, I was able to start running again and doing my daily work. My military education at Fort Leavenworth paved the way for my promotion to major of the US Army. It was not long before my promotion was announced. I received my rank as major of the US Army at the main post chapel, the chapel of my congregation. My wife, my son, my 509th ABN commander, and my commanding chaplain helped to pin my rank. Friends and loved ones from my unit, the chapels, and my congregation came to celebrate with me. Leth prepared something for us to eat and drink for this celebration. It was a solemn, quiet, and good one.

Traditionally, after a higher rank is awarded, new responsibility follows. I received a new order to go to Fort McPherson. I didn't know much about Fort McPherson, but those who knew the system well told me I was getting a prestigious job. I found out that the place I was going to was the home of one of the higher-ranking officers of the US Army. The new job of resource manager was far from my interest, and the more I learned about the job, the more uncomfortable I became. However, I was told that I would go for training to learn my job. That was very comforting.

Chapter 12

Atlanta Tour and the Symptoms

I anticipated the move with mixed excitement and fear. Leth felt the same way. She always wanted to move to a bigger city, like Atlanta, and she anticipated that there would be a new opportunity that would come my way. However, we were concerned about being so far from Diwang. He was already in college, and occasionally he came home on weekends, when he needed laundry, when he was short of money, or for whatever reason. This move would be just for Leth and me.

My new salary was an increase, but the unsold house that we were leaving behind would just eat up that increase as well as our savings. We also had to look for a new house. With every move, it seemed like buying a house was more appealing than renting one. But the pain was great when we had to leave and no one bought our house as fast as we expected. That was exactly what happened in Leesville. There was no buyer at the time we moved, so we ended up renting the house again just to avoid losing our savings.

This time we thought we were smarter by renting a house. It was a good house in a good neighborhood. Unfortunately, after a year, the owner gave us notice that we could not renew our lease because the owner's son wanted to move in. So we ended up buying a house again in the same neighborhood, in Jonesboro, Georgia. We decided that buying would prevent us from the hassle of moving from one house to another on a yearly basis, especially if we were to pay our own expenses. I had to ask my relatives to help me, my kids, and my son-in-law.

After getting settled, Leth started to look for a job. Since she was interested in clinical pastoral education, the presence of Emory

University and the hospital renewed her interest in serving as a chaplain in a hospital setting. The move was stressful. Leth was acting strange. She was getting irritated and forgetting things, and she was very sensitive to comments. The nice thing was that she was aware of this. It made it easier for me to advise her to seek professional help.

Her menstruation stopped, and she assumed it was due to her stress level. When she applied for her CPE, she didn't wait long to be accepted. I thought this would probably help her feel worthy and useful and boost her self-esteem, but it did not help. She came home frustrated and sometimes crying. She forgot things and felt so embarrassed among her colleagues. Her supervisor noticed these patterns of behavior and asked her to see a doctor, which she did.

Dr. Abelara, a female Filipino doctor with Fort McPherson Clinic, was the first doctor she went to see. Leth and I described her recent behavior, and Dr. Abelara thought it seemed normal for women whose menstruation had stopped. However, she referred her to a neurologist, Dr. Noggin, a civilian doctor outside the military setting. Dr. Noggin's test showed that she had a mild cognitive impairment (MCI).

Leth started taking estrogen and medication for memory. Sometimes I could see progress, but other times I felt it was getting worse. She would forget where she parked the car, what hospital ward she was supposed to go for duty, where her purse or keys were, etc. Since I also had these moments of forgetfulness, I just assumed that it wasn't that serious. She was still functional and could do lots of things, so I just ignored all the symptoms. I thought we would just keep her busy and therapy would be good for her.

We were both busy. I left her and went to military school to learn my resource manager job, which consisted of managing money and the chapels' properties, and looking for other resources to keep all the chapels functional. The chapels that I was managing as resource manager of the garrison were: Fort Gillem, Fort McPherson, and the unit chapels in Arab countries that we were associated with. The resource manager trainer helped, but it was different when I started to work in the real world. Fortunately, the army gave me some soldiers experienced with that particular job. The greatest asset was having the paid professional civilian resource manager on hand who oversaw the work of the entire 5th Army. When I encountered problems, it was easy for me to call her for help.

I became the deputy chaplain of the Garrison Chapel. Whenever the senior chaplain was gone, I took charge. The chapels at the main post were attended not only by on-post soldiers but also by many retirees, some of whom were high-ranking US Army officers. The protestant chapel was not that big, but almost every Sunday we had a fairly good number of worship attendees. The Sunday school was well attended, and the prayer breakfast for men was the same. We had a complete team of staff to help us do our job: a secretary, a staff sergeant, a corporal, a specialist, a Christian education coordinator, and numerous volunteers.

After two years, there was concern that there weren't enough major officers to fill the vacancies in the army. The combat units were the priority. Since I was major officer, I was asked to move to Fort Hood and fill the Red Team position as brigade chaplain. I liked my job in Fort McPherson; it was enjoyable and prestigious. Even though I was not the main post chaplain or in charge of the post chapel, I felt like I was doing a very significant job that I really liked. Mingling with higher-rank officers, not playing in the mud like I did in the combat unit, and not experiencing separation from my family while training really spoiled me.

City life was very meaningful to my wife also. We both joined the choir and enjoyed it so much. On weekends, we drove around, ate out, went to Stone Mountain, went downtown, saw plays, and just enjoyed the Atlanta area and all the scenic views and points of interest that it offered. But we both knew that this tour wouldn't last forever. When the army told us to move, we did and assumed that this was part of God's greater plan for us.

When we heard the news, I thought my wife would be hesitant. She must have been getting used to the system. She asked, "Where are we going this time?"

I said, "Fort Hood, Texas, the largest US Army base in the world." I thought we would stay here for three years, but here we went again, getting ready to move. We stayed in our new house for just a year and we were already moving to Texas. Since we liked Atlanta and the new house we bought, we decided to keep it for our retirement. We also found out that there were more potential renters in the area, so it worked in our favor not to sell the house but to open it up for rent.

Amazingly, right after our moving announcement, many realtors in Texas were showering us with offers to sell us a house. The army allowed us to visit and see the place we were going to buy or rent. As usual, we had to ponder again if we needed to buy or rent a house. Most of the houses were not our taste. We didn't want to buy a house since we already had one that we liked in Atlanta. Furthermore, it took a while for us to sell our house in Louisiana, and we lost lots of money when we sold it.

After three days of looking for places to rent, we did not find any that we really liked. Leth and I drove around and saw a house for sale that was built of stone. It was nice and in a good neighborhood. We took the brochure displayed in front of the house, and it seemed affordable—less than $100,000. Comparing the cost of renting and the monthly payment, we thought this would be a great deal. We looked inside and outside the house. It was a dream house for us. Leth and I fell in love with the house, especially when we found out that many officers were living in the same neighborhood.

We decided to buy the house but agreed that would sell our house in Jonesboro, Georgia. But before the house in Georgia was placed for sale, a family wanted to rent it, so we settled for that. As Leth continued to prepare for the big move, she was tried to finish up her CPE as well as some of her medical tests. Dr. Abelara's evaluation was confirmed by her neurologist: there was a clear pattern of dementia in Leth's behavior. She started taking medication for dementia. It was becoming more and more obvious that she was suffering from short-term memory loss. Her supervisor confronted her about her mild cognitive impairment during her CPE class. Her colleagues made the same observation. One day when I went to pick her up, she broke down and cried and asked me, "Why is this happening to me?"

The nice thing, I discovered, was that after a while she forgot all that had happened. She started planning things without any worries or any consideration for her health. I was worried about her condition. Her positive attitude, on the other hand, helped me overcome some of my worries, though I worried sometimes about her positive attitude as part of her sickness. At times I took advantage of her short-term memory. Whenever I made her upset or we had some misunderstanding, I just waited for a moment, changed the subject, and she quickly forgot what happened. I thought that was good and very advantageous for me. Sometimes I just told myself, "Thank you, Lord, I have been forgiven."

As the moving day got closer, Leth was so stressed that she could not make up her mind about what she would and would not pack. She would put things in a box and then start unpacking again, which stressed me out. Sometimes I forgot about her sickness, and with frustration I would start screaming, "Make up your mind! What is it that you really want?" Then she would start crying and feeling sorry for herself, like she was no longer useful to me. This exchange of words went on and on. Sometimes I said things I didn't mean and she did the same, which strained our relationship.

There were times I had to get away to compose myself, and when I came back, she met me with a smile, as if nothing happened. In a way, it helped me remember that I was dealing with my wife who had dementia. The move was tough for me, but I managed and learned to keep telling myself that I needed to make the adjustment.

At times, I got frustrated thinking that she was playing a game with me. She could remember lots of things that happened two or three weeks ago and all our years together in Europe. I wondered why she could remember those things but could not remember what happened just an hour or a minute ago. It was strange, but I was told that it was due to her sickness. It started with short-term memory loss and then long-term memory until she forgot everything completely.

I couldn't help but go, run, and cry, thinking of what she was becoming. I prayed to God to help me prepare for everything that was coming. Perhaps it was God's plan that we would go to Fort Hood as the coming of my separation from the US Army approached. The idea of being a brigade chaplain and in charge of a chapel with several chaplains working for me became an ego booster for me. This meant that it would be a good job for me, because I would be working with the chaplains in the chapel and in the field. I would also be working with multiple staff within the brigade system. Leth planned to take a break, stay home, and take care of herself and me. I thought that was a good plan.

Chapter 13

Fort Hood, Texas

Welcome to Fort Hood, Texas, the home of two divisions and the largest US Army base in the United States. We liked our new home, I liked my new job, and so with Leth. She seemed to like our new area. In between work, I tried to help Leth get settled with unpacking and arranging our household goods and putting them where they belonged. The units of my brigade were so mobile and always on the move, training, training, training. I was back again with the artillery unit, not with the battalion, but now I was with the brigade, the Red Team of the 1st Cavalry Division.

The brigade had four battalions and another three attached to me because they had no chaplain. The job was like a 180-degree turn. I was supervising a larger group of chaplains and chaplain assistants. I had more personnel to work with, more meetings to attend, more paperwork, and more battalion coverage. The job varied, and it was never boring. For two years I did not go to the field, but now I could go and visit our soldiers. The job was exciting because it gave me a greater perspective of and appreciation for how the military system worked in all its complexity.

The technology we used in combat was amazing, and it continued to change as we embraced the high-tech computer age. To keep updated, everyone in the military must be computer literate. I didn't like it, and I was kind of scared of the computer, but now that I got into it, I could no longer work without one. Computer programs today can be obsolete after six months or a year. The best way for me to learn was just by getting on the computer, working, and asking questions until I got it right. I became computer literate because of the US Army.

After a month, Leth found out that it was not her way to just stay home, as she had planned before we arrived in Fort Hood, Texas. She started to look for work and came across one of the hospitals with a CPE program. She wanted to complete her year of CPE training. She applied and was accepted. I thought it would be good to let her keep busy and do something that she enjoyed. Sometimes when I was in the field with my soldiers, I thought she would be okay, but one day she called me up and sounded so scared because she could not find her way home.

I was in the field and it was already late in the afternoon when she called me. She said that she came from work in Temple, Texas, and was heading home. She had been driving for a while and probably missed her exit. I tried to calm her down and asked her what she saw on the street signs, so she described what she saw. The place was familiar to me, so I told her to turn around because she was heading to Austin. I tried to guide her by staying on the phone with her. Then we lost contact, probably because her cell phone had a low battery. My brigade XO was considerate and he allowed me to go home and stay with my wife. When I reached home, I found that her car was already there and she said she just got home. She found her way home by stopping at every store or gas station and asking directions. It took a while, but she made it home.

Her experience was scary for me. I told her to quit her job, but she didn't like the idea. I tried to be as supportive as I could. I took her again to see a doctor on post. Since there was no neurologist, she was referred to one outside the military clinic. After all her tests, this neurologist told us that she had MCI indeed, and it was an early stage of dementia, called Alzheimer's disease. Since the doctor worked at the same hospital where she was taking her CPE, Leth's supervisor found this out and told her that it would be for her own good to get healed first before she pursued her CPE program.

Leth knew then that it would be her last opportunity to get a job before school. She fought for it and believed that prayer would cure her. She prayed a lot and so did I. We went to see another doctor for a second opinion, but the result was the same. One day, I asked her to come to my office and help me organize my room. She drove her car and followed me. After she was done unpacking some of my books, she decided to go home and cook our lunch. Our home was just five miles away from the base. I was so busy that I did not go home for lunch on time.

I was twenty or thirty minutes late when I went home, and her car was not there yet. As I got out from my car, I saw her coming. She was smiling at first, but then she started crying and told me that she was lost and could not find her way back home. She was able to get home only because she kept on asking people how to get to Harker Heights, our village. When she saw some familiar places, she knew she was on her way home. What could I do except comfort and embrace her. She was apologetic for not cooking our lunch, but I told her that leftovers would do just fine.

What was happening started to worry me again, and I began wondering what God's plan was for us. If this continued and got worse, as the doctors predicted, what would become of the military? I started feeling chest pains, and my doctors continued to monitor my case. My cardiologist put in my profile that I could not be deployed unless there was a cardiologist deployed in that area. At that time I started talking to Leth about going back to the local church ministry, the Iowa Conference. Leth thought that was a great idea, and she herself could go back to the ministry and get her ordination.

As we thought about this, 9/11 hit the country. I was in my office when my chaplain assistants started screaming that the Twin Towers in New York were destroyed by an airplane. Not long after the incident, the president of the United States declared war against the terrorists. All of us were on alert. The security on post became so intense that we had to wake up really early in the morning to get on post. Within that week we started deploying people to Afghanistan and Iraq. We were on alert to be deployed anytime we were needed. Suddenly, all evaluations were set aside, and it came out that I could not be deployed. The brigade needed to replace me as soon as possible, and the Chaplain Corps had to decide where to put me so that the replacement chaplain could get in.

Since my profile was being evaluated, I chose to be released and go back to the parish pastorate. I notified my bishop of the Iowa Conference about my desire to go back to Iowa. It was timely because the conference year and appointment system were coming. Kuya Eming informed me of what was happening in the conference, since he was one of the district superintendents. He told me that if I needed to come back, this was the time to do it.

As the soldiers geared up for deployment to Afghanistan and Iraq, I was pulled out from the Red Team and put in the hospital setting to take care of the soldiers and families who were hospitalized. While doing the hospital chaplain's work, I was also busy working on my paper for release. The process took longer than I thought. I found out that they were not in a hurry to release me because they needed chaplains to work in the hospital. The senior chaplain made me his deputy. After much correspondence back and forth between the Chaplain Corps and the United Methodist Church cabinet of the Iowa Conference, the date of my release order finally came.

Being a military hospital chaplain was a good experience too. I was glad that happened prior to my leaving the US Army. It was a good experience to work with doctors and medical staff. It also gave me lots of time to learn about my wife's disease. What happened seemed to work in my favor. As I reflected upon my experience with Leth, I realized I could no longer leave my wife if I were to be deployed. I knew that my wife would not get better if I stayed in the military.

While waiting for my release order, the Iowa Conference cabinet was making my appointment. Good news finally came when the district superintendent of the Dubuque district asked me if I would accept their first choice for me, my church appointment—First United Methodist Church in Maquoketa, Iowa. The church was not that small, but in the Dubuque district it was considered fairly large with more than five hundred individual members. The salary was lower than what I received from the military. However, it was a decent salary for the Iowa Conference. I was told that my experience and seniority as a member of the Iowa Conference was taken into consideration in this appointment. With all these considerations, I accepted this appointment as a blessing and without hesitancy.

I could not believe I was moving again. This time I was moving from the military to a civilian life. Unfortunately, I did not have enough years to retire. The 10 percent point I was given for my medical health profile was not enough to qualify for retirement due to a medical reason. I was awarded only for health compensation and separation. The Veterans Administration was more gracious when they awarded me 70 percent to begin with, and at later date I was granted 100 percent.

The pastor I was replacing was retiring, and I had to wait more than a month before I could move into the house that the church was providing for Leth and me. As usual, the problem arose of selling the house we had just bought. Fortunately, my compensation was good enough to pay for the whole house, which I paid in full so that I did not have to worry about my monthly loan payments. After his graduation, my son took care of the monthly mortgage of our house in Georgia.

We felt God was watching and guiding us in every plan and movement we made. The army helped me move my household goods and held them in Davenport until I was ready to move into our new Iowa home. While in transition, my daughter offered us her house in Wisconsin until we got into our new home. Meanwhile, we took advantage of the travel and saw some places before we got to Wisconsin. I thought the US Army would be my professional career, but somehow, for many good reasons, I ended up back at the parish ministry. I was no longer certain of anything about our future, except to trust that God would always work in my favor.

Chapter 14

Back to Parish Ministry

It was great to see Iowa again. We first went to see the church and meet the Staff/Pastor-Parish Relations Committee (SPPRC). It had been a while since I had heard or seen a SPPRC. I had left the local church almost fourteen years ago, and since then I had not dealt with any bureaucratic system of the church. Now, I was back and ready to face the old system I left. There had been some changes in the church polity but not much. The SPPRC was very cordial and made it easy for me to express myself. They did a good job of welcoming me in their first meeting. My wife and I were very pleased.

We also had the chance to see the parsonage, and Leth's first reaction was that it was too small. I guessed she was used to staying in spacious houses of her choice, but now we had no choice except to take whatever parsonage the church had to offer. I told her to learn to adjust and to get rid of some of the toys she had acquired when we were in the military.

When my predecessor left, we moved in quickly from Wisconsin and occupied the parsonage. The mover was also notified to bring in our household goods. It was unbelievable how much junk we had accumulated. We just didn't have enough room to put some of our furniture. We started to give some of it away to our kids, friends, and relatives. Still the garage was full, and there was no other storage in the parsonage. The house had three small bedrooms, one and a half bathrooms, and one full basement.

Leth's short-term memory loss was getting more and more obvious, and many members started to notice. But she had not changed anything about her social life. She was always involved in church activities. This got her and me into trouble when she started making commitments but forgot them. At the parsonage, she unpacked boxes, got distracted, and then opened another box but didn't know what to do with it. The house ended up messy every time I came home. And even though I was tired, I tried to make the house presentable, because we had many members who were eager to come and see the new pastor in town.

She always enjoyed company, and members began to like her, so I warned some of them that she was not healthy. Leth was mad when she found out that I was telling members about her sickness. I tried to reason with her, because eventually members would find out with the way she had been acting. Reasoning with her did not help our relationship at all. However, those members who had learned about her illness were more sensitive and helpful when they were dealing with her. Furthermore, we had some active members who were working or volunteering at the nursing home.

Leth became more and more suspicious of me. She thought I was telling members that she was crazy, and she started isolating herself from the church. Fortunately, we had some members who worked with cases like hers, so they were both supportive of and helpful to Leth and me. Some members tried to get her involved with the prayer group and choir. The nice thing was that she forgot what she was mad about, and when they got her to some activities, she seemed excited and she enjoyed the event.

One day, when I came home from work, Leth told me that she wanted to visit her relatives in Chicago. She thought about her sister, Eunice, and so she called her. Eunice complained about her living situation, being far from relatives, and the dangerous area in which she lived because of the drug dealers. I overheard Leth offer her to come and be with her. Eunice got so excited, and she wanted to come right away. Leth told me to talk to her. They both already had it planned. Since Leth was no longer working, they would have lots of time to be together. I thought that this was a good plan. Both of them could help and entertain each other, and I would have nothing to worry about when I was at work. I even promised that I would give Eunice pocket money.

I thought the plan was great until I got a call from Leth's other sisters accusing me of manipulating and taking advantage of Eunice. Our good intention went sour. I never saw my wife so angry in my entire life. She had lost words of reason, and all she could do was yell and scream at the phone. She thought that her two sisters were conspiring against her. She banged the phone down with so much frustration, because she could no longer express herself except by crying and screaming. I tried to calm her down, give her time and space, and let her talk while I just stayed with her and listened.

I suggested that perhaps it would be better to return Eunice back to Joliet, Illinois, because her presence was causing more stress to her and creating conflict within her family. Leth was furious when I said that. Eunice said that she wanted to stay with us and with her sister. Furthermore, she felt like she was more secure with us than in Joliet. She told us that when she needed help, her other sister was always busy, and when she was hospitalized her sister just came at her convenience. They did not come to see her regularly, and she felt lonely. She also felt that she was called only when she was needed to take care of her nephew.

Leth and Eunice seemed to bond, especially when Eunice told her all the negative things she could think of about her two sisters. That was exactly what Leth wanted to hear at that time, of course, because of the existing conflict between her and her sisters. But after a while, Eunice started to miss all the social security benefits she had been getting from the state of Illinois. The amount I promised her was not enough. She started comparing it to what she was receiving in Illinois and discovered that she would get those benefits only if she applied in the state of Iowa and had her own apartment.

Meanwhile, Leth and Eunice's relationship was getting strained due to Leth's suspicious attitude, which was a part of Leth's growing sickness. Leth suspected Eunice was flirting with me. She suspected she was stealing her clothes and jewelry and anything she could think of. She accused Eunice of so many things that, of course, Eunice did not do. I found Eunice crying and feeling uncomfortable. I had to explain to her many times that Leth's attitude was part of her sickness and that all she needed to do was distract her by changing the topic and everything would be forgotten. I even taught her how to do it, and it worked. But, of course, Eunice was not mentally healthy either, so everything started getting on her nerves. Eunice seemed to communicate all of this to her sisters, which did not help the relationship because somehow Leth found out.

When Eunice got her apartment, it was a good break for her, but then Leth started to miss her sister and she called her. The problem was that when they were together, Leth would say things that Eunice took seriously, so Eunice started to get depressed again. However, Eunice seemed to understand the pattern of her sisters' behavior, but there were also times that she was depressed and let the negative thoughts eat at her. This back-and-forth bickering between the two of them started to affect my health. I even talked to Eunice about how she felt about going back to Illinois, but she seemed to like her place and the fact that it was near the clinic and the hospital. She even said, "I would stay here in Maquoketa, forever." However, I knew Eunice would change her mind, and she did. She even commented that, since moving to Maquoketa, she had never been hospitalized, unlike in Illinois.

I had been in and out of the clinic for continued checkups. I was even hospitalized several times because of some irregularities of my heartbeat as well as some chest pain. It was recommended that I see a psychiatrist due to the major stresses in my life. The situation at home and my health did not get better. Leth's case slowly got worse, and it was obvious. Once I came home and the whole kitchen was smoking. Leth was cooking unattended. Perhaps she was distracted and went to the bedroom and slept. This happened more than once and it started to worry me. I felt secure when Eunice was around, but there were times Leth didn't want Eunice to be around. Her mood kept on changing, which created more confusion for Eunice.

There were times Eunice was critical of her, and Leth said she was treated like a kid. In a way, Leth often acted like a kid, because it was the nature of her sickness. However, patients like her may have childish behaviors, but many patients still insisted on keeping their dignity and being treated like they used to be. Eunice got so depressed, too, so I had to attend to her, explain over and over again the nature of her sister's sickness, and remind her not to take her so seriously. Both of them were mentally unstable, and with my busy schedule in the church, as well as taking care of my own health, it became too much for me to handle.

My doctor's appointments became more and more regular until someone told me to see a counselor for myself. At first I was hesitant, perhaps because of my own ego. I knew in my heart the importance of seeing a counselor, because I had counseled lots of soldiers and families, and many had been helped. I thought I knew my problems and could resolve them by myself, but I couldn't. I finally gave in and sought out a fellow counselor, someone who was professionally known and had been a pastor himself. A district superintendent of the United Methodist Church recommended someone who had been a counselor and came highly respected by clergy in the Iowa Conference.

I didn't know the man, but I felt confident that he was someone I could relate to. After several psychological tests, he sent the results to me as well as to my district superintendent. The test was very detailed. I had to carefully prioritize and make plans. With my wife's dementia slowly robbing her life and future, and with my heart problems (five bypass surgeries and constant chest pain, etc.), I could not really do my professional work well anymore. In a way, I would not be doing justice to the church I was supposed to serve, since I was spending more and more time going to the doctors and had been hospitalized twice within a year.

I was grateful that there were so many gifted leaders in our church who, in my absence, provided ministries, but this would not be a good reason to take advantage of it. With so many issues to consider, I started contemplating leaving the ministry. The question was: could I afford it? Maybe not! But I knew eventually my wife would be in a nursing home and I would end up in the hospital, too, if I did not take care of my health. The church was not that small, and it demanded a ministry greater than I could provide due to my health. My counselor warned me that if I continued on this path, I would have another heart attack. With prayerful consideration, I finally talked to my district superintendent and told him that I was considering leaving the pastorate.

I had to explain how I came to that decision. At first he tried to be supportive and keep me, but I had already made up my mind. He seemed to understand, especially when he received the letter from my counselor. I told the DS that I wanted to spend quality time with my wife in her remaining years while we could still enjoy each other and before she ended up in a nursing home. This time he seemed supportive and gave me his blessing. As expected, I had to go through every committee channel in the church system before I could get the church's complete blessing.

The church members and I were concerned about our financial status once I would no longer be working in the church. Carefully I had calculated the money I was receiving from my VA Disability Comp and my wife's social security. The total amount was not that great, but it would help us get by. I started processing my exit from the active church ministry. I was encouraged to apply for disability insurance through the United Methodist Church Board of Pension and through the Social Security Administration. A VA representative also helped me apply for more, 100 percent disability compensation. Friends and loved ones were helpful and supportive as we went through the process of leaving and applying for all these possible benefits that could help us.

For a while, my wife and I lived on our savings, with very limited income. All our disability insurance was approved. The approval did not come that easily. We had to wait for a while. We even used a lawyer to help me get a social security benefit before it was approved. With God's abounding love and mercy, our prayer was answered and we got approved, not in the time we wanted but at the later date.

Meanwhile, when we started processing that we were leaving the pastorate, Eunice became so restless. She felt very sick and told me she wanted to be confined in the hospital. I took her to the hospital, and they found nothing wrong with her. Her counselor told us that she was stressed because she claimed that we took her to Maquoketa and now we were abandoning her. She had a great life in Illinois, and now she felt miserable and it was our fault. She told this, not just to her counselor, but also to some church members and relatives. We probably looked bad to some people, but we explained our side to those who really took the time to find out our plan.

We were moving to North Liberty to be close to my daughter because I would need Amy's help when emergencies arose. Eunice could come with us if she wanted too. She told us that she wanted to stay in Maquoketa forever and that it was an ideal place for her. We did not bother her about coming with us. However, we told her that she would be welcome if she wanted to come with us to North Liberty, and then she started to inquire about the possibilities. At times she would say that she would come, and then at times she would say it was better for her just to stay there.

Before leaving the church, we had the chance to visit Europe on an educational cruise, "Paul's 4th Missionary Journey" led by the three bishops, including the Iowa bishop, Gregory Palmer. I took my mom, Eunice, and Leth on this trip. It was a great experience for all of us, especially for Leth since she had been dreaming to go to these places. My mom and Eunice never had this kind of journey before, so it was very meaningful to both of them. Eunice was very appreciative, since we took care of her fare. At the beginning, my mother was hesitant to come due to the high cost. However, after her awesome experience, she was very thankful.

Packing time came again, and we got ready to move to our newly bought home, a condominium in North Liberty. Since Leth and I could no longer do lots of maintenance in a big house, a small three-room condo would be the right size for us. This meant that we had to get rid of more furniture and other things that we had accumulated over several years. We got rid of our stuff by having garage sales and giving things away to friends and relatives. We even called the United Methodist Camp at Pictured Rocks and had them haul away our furniture and electronics. But still there was plenty that we hauled to North Liberty.

When we left Maquoketa, we first went to the Philippines because the condo we bought was not ready for at least three to six months. We had to store all our things in the condo's two-car garage. Leth wanted to see her brothers and sisters while she could still remember them and talk to them. So we first went to Iloilo to see her brother Valeriano Jr. and his family, and then to Manila to see her sister and other brothers. The visit was both rewarding and confusing for Leth. There were times she didn't understand why we were there, and there were times she knew why we were there. It was the same when she wanted to see Peking, China. It was a mix of joyful and confusing experiences for her. She was excited to go and see the place, but then she was upset with me and wondered why I took her there. She even accused me of tormenting her with all the traveling.

It occurred to me that constant change was not a good idea for Leth. I learned my lesson the hard way. She began to feel at peace when we finally settled in Maria Aurora, Aurora, at my sister's house. We were just there temporarily. The moving began again when we left the Philippines and went back to the States to get settled in our new condo in North Liberty. My wife was confused about what was happening, but I could not help it. It was hard for me as well, especially when we arrived in the States. We had to stay at Amy's house while we were in the process of finalizing documents and transferring the condo to our name.

Settling into the condo was a great relief for me, but with Leth's progression of dementia, it was just temporary. However, I saw how secure she felt when we started to settle; it gave her the assurance that this place was really our home. From time to time she would ask me to take her home, and over and over again I told her that this place was really our home. I was so stressed out that I got sick several times and had to see my doctors. I knew that a support group helped me a lot when I joined in Maquoketa, so I went again and found another support group in Iowa City. I found a good one and attended to help me with my sanity.

Chapter 15

Disability Life

There we were back in North Liberty, Iowa, no longer in a parsonage but in our new three-bedroom condominium. I thought this would be our last move. We continued to downsize, but our garage was still full of junk. We still needed to get rid of our baggage. I continued to give things away without Leth's approval. I knew she would keep it all if she could, so I had learned not to show her anything. The irony was that we got rid of some of our furniture, but now we started to buy new furniture that matched our condo. We also needed some personal items for the sake of Leth's safety.

Since we moved to another new community, I had to take Leth again to another new doctor. The university hospital clinic was our first choice, so we were referred to a new neurologist. Going to the doctor was a big challenge, because Leth did not trust doctors and did not like to see them. There was no way I could convince her to go to the doctor. Sometimes I had to tell lies, like "Let us go to the park and go fishing." This way I could make her come with me and then take her to the doctor. Once we got to the doctor's office, some staff had ways of easing her apprehensions.

Keeping our small apartment in order was not that easy. There were times Leth opened the closet or drawers but didn't know how to put them back. Sometimes the clean clothes and the dirty clothes were put together in the same place. Sometimes food was in the closet and hair combs were in the refrigerator. She would wash the dishes, but then the clean and dirty ones were mixed together. There were times I got so stressed that my voice started to raise and I said things that were not appropriate for her to hear. She would start crying, screaming, hitting her head, and saying "I am better off dead." Or sometimes she would say, "I am no longer useful to you!" or "Let me die!" or "Just leave me now and divorce me!"

Once I heard all these comments, it helped me to come to my senses and remind me that I was dealing with a woman who had dementia. There were times I had to calm down, shut up, and just listen to her. Once she started quieting down, I would wait for a few moments, and then I would just try to change the topic. After a while everything was forgotten, and I just assumed I too was forgiven. I could tell by her facial expression that she did not know what had happened. However, there were times too that I just lost control. I could not find peace within myself because of all my anger. But the fact remained that there was not much I could do except calm my voice and cool off.

Fishing was therapeutic for me. North Liberty was just five miles from Coralville Lake. Fortunately, when we arrived in North Liberty was when the fish were starting to bite. The stripers and white bass were biting like crazy, so I had fun and went fishing almost every morning. I had to wake up at four thirty in the morning while Leth was still deeply asleep, and then I came back when Leth was about to wake up. There were many times I had caught plenty of fish, but there were also times I had just enough for lunch or dinner. This experience was probably the most rewarding. I enjoyed each day and found fishing very therapeutic.

My daughter sometimes brought the kids for us to watch, and at times it was very entertaining for Leth and me. We played with the kids and saw them more often. Ashtin started to go to day care, and Leth seemed to enjoy whenever we went to get her from school. Her presence really helped Leth. When Tre, our grandson, was born, that added a joy in our lives. I enjoyed their presence, and Leth was having a good time too, unless Ashtin started screaming when she got excited or when the baby cried at length. Loud noise and screaming kids often bothered Leth. At one time, Leth was just so upset and went to our room covering her ears. I told Ashtin, "Don't scream, honey, your *lola* has only one ear." (*Lola* means "grandma" in the Filipino language.) Ashtin ran to see *Lola* and then came back and said, "Lola has two ears,

Lolo, come and see!" (*Lolo* means "grandpa" in the Filipino language.) All I could do was smile and explain what I meant.

Leth loved it when I drove her around North Liberty, Coralville, and Iowa City. And when Amy brought us the kids, we did the same thing. We would drive around the area and go to parks, and Leth and Ashtin would play while I pushed Tre around in the stroller. But at times it was not that much fun for me because I had to take care of not only the kids but also Leth. However, Amy and Richard helped us by taking us around, and we used this as our family time. We had chosen Amy's church so that we could be together as a family. When Amy took the job as a youth pastor of the Coralville United Methodist Church, we too joined and started to establish a support group in the Sunday school classes.

Leth also got involved in the university program, where students were asked to do community service. Volunteer students would watch the patients for a few hours to give their caregivers time to get their chores done without worrying or having to watch their loved ones with dementia. The program went well for me, but not for my wife when she started accusing the volunteers of touching sensitive parts of her body. Every time she saw one student, she got angry and very upset.

My daughter and I talked to the student supervisor and mentioned my wife's accusation and reactions. The supervisor said that she knew the student had a good record. They found no such record of sexual molestation from this student. But for the sake of the patient's peace of mind as well as the student, the student was removed from our case. Leth's sexual accusation was unfortunately common among people who had dementia. It was clear in their mind that the event occurred even if it did not. It was a good program, but it probably was not meant for us.

Whenever I went shopping, I had to watch my wife. There were times I told her just to stay at the bench and wait for me while I shopped. At first she was able to manage that, but later she could no longer stay and wait. Sometimes she had to stay in the car and wait for me, especially when I was just going to buy one item and would come back quickly. But this strategy did not last long either, because one time when

I got back she was not in the car. It took almost a half hour to find her. She said, "I needed to go to the bathroom, but then when I got back you were gone." She was very upset with me. The truth was that I was not gone; she just could not remember how to get back to the car.

One of the Alzheimer's support group members had the same problems I experienced. The group suggested that perhaps a wheelchair would help. I thought that would be a great idea for Leth. Since she used to love window-shopping and going out for a walk, this would help me have some control. I wouldn't have to bother watching her all the time. If she was in a wheelchair, we could shop together and go for a stroll, since she walked very, very slowly. I went quickly and started shopping for a wheelchair. The good news was that I could get it for free as long as her doctor supported the idea. Fortunately, the doctor agreed 100 percent. So I was highly encouraged and went to get one.

I thought this would be a good proposition for Leth, but her reaction was so intense that she started yelling at me and telling me I was treating her like a handicapped person. She said, "As long as I can still walk, I will never ride in a wheelchair. I am not handicapped. Why? Are you tired of me? If you don't want me anymore, let me know and I will just leave."

I had to pray about how I could explain the benefit of the wheelchair. She would not listen. Again I lost control and my voice went louder than hers. Amazingly she did not say anything. She seemed scared, so I immediately embraced her and said, "I'm sorry, honey, I don't mean to yell at you. I'm just trying to do something that will make my life and yours easier. I am doing this for both of us."

Then she said, "Then, when can we get this?"

Often her reactions seemed like a contradiction. One minute she would be willing to do something and then a minute later she would resist doing the same thing she had been willing to do. But as she used the wheelchair more often then, it became easier for her to forget all the resistance she had shown during the first few weeks. When we were ready to go out, she just automatically sat in her wheelchair. It made it easier for me to control where she wandered around, and we were able to move faster. The wheelchair was a blessing indeed for both of us. I worried less about her getting lost and falling down.

Meanwhile, Amy and Richard did not think that they were making any progress financially. They were hurt financially when they moved to Iowa from Wisconsin and could not sell their log cabin. As a result, they were forced to sell their home at a loss of more than $40,000. They chose to borrow money to help them pay for their loss rather than apply for bankruptcy. Richard discovered that the business he thought would work didn't, because his partner was not honest enough to tell him what was going on, and this forced him to leave the partnership. He went to work with the bank, but unfortunately his income was not enough to pay for the basics. Amy started to look for the same job she used to do, and job hunting went a lot easier.

Amy accepted an interview to see if she would like the job. We all went to Athens, Georgia, and Amy accepted the job. The location was perfect for Leth and me, I thought, because it was close to Diwang. It fulfilled our dream to have our whole family close to each other. We looked around the city and found a nice home where we would possibly live. Instead of buying two houses, we decided to buy just one big house. Richard thought it would be a great idea to stay together rather than buy two houses and maintain both. Privacy was important to both of us, so we had to consider that if we were to buy a house. A duplex could be an ideal possibility. The realtor was a church member, and he was kind enough to show us possible houses that were big enough for our requirements but within budget.

Finally, we found the house that we really liked. It was an affordable duplex. The first floor in the front of the house would be our home. The basement would be Amy's family home. Each floor was the same size, except the basement kitchen was not as complete as ours. We went back to Iowa and started to pack again and plan for another big move. We were hesitant to move, but it seemed that we did not have much choice. I needed my children to help me take care of my wife. The move to North Liberty, I thought, would be the last one. Now I couldn't believe how fast another change had come.

Aleta

We put our condo on the market, but unfortunately in our location there were many condos and single family homes for sale. It would be hard to compete and sell our condo unless we really went down in price. We put the house on the market, and only a few people came to see it. But no one made an offer. As the moving date got closer, we offered the house for rent. Before we moved, there was a customer who wanted to rent the condo, so we went ahead and made arrangements before we moved. Our condo was removed from the market and became a rental property.

Chapter 16

Georgia Life

Again, the move was another confusing experience for Leth. She did not understand why so many people came to our home to help us move. At times, she tried to be helpful but instead it was more disastrous. She would open a box that was already sealed for travel. Or sometimes she would see some of our kitchen equipment in a box and would remove it, for fear that someone would take it. She was suspicious of those who came to help us. I kept trying to give away our leftover household goods to friends and relatives. The house we were moving to in Georgia was larger, but the storage was minimal.

We became highly selective of what we would bring. If we had duplicate tools, we had to keep whatever was newer and better. We had a garage sale to get rid of all the winter tools that we did not need in the South, the clothes that Leth had outgrown, and the formal clothes that she had worn for all our military balls. We had to keep Leth away from the garage sale, because when she saw her things she wanted to gather them all back. She said, "These are all mine. Don't take what is mine." I felt bad doing this to her, but I knew she would not need these items anymore, and it was better if someone else could use them. Our relatives took some of her expensive clothes, and I was glad.

I hired the biggest "Budget Truck" to haul my household goods. My relatives from Chicago came to help. Amy's things were hauled separately, since her employer was moving her for free. Unfortunately, I still had plenty of junk that I needed to get rid of. I gave away some of it and threw out the rest. Some of my colorful stones were accidentally thrown out. Diwang thought they were trash, but those were expensive and treasures for us. Perhaps this was the award for moving. We always lost and misplaced things that we treasured.

It was late in the afternoon when we fully loaded the moving truck. We left Iowa and had to travel that hot afternoon. Richard had to drive the truck, and Amy drove my Cadillac because it was large enough for baby Tre, Ashtin, and my brother, Boyet's kids. Juanito, my other brother and his girlfriend, Marlene joined us on our way to Illinois assisting Rich in driving. Boyet's family came along to help, not just in moving, but also as drivers for our extra cars. It was hot that day, and the car's air-conditioning helped. Unfortunately, the air conditioner in Richard's truck was broken, and he had to suffer that long, hot way from Iowa to Georgia.

We arrived at our new address: 269 Hampton Park Drive, Athens, Georgia. Would this be our last move? I knew we might stay longer here because Amy seemed committed to stay for the sake of the kids' schooling. We would have loved to stay permanently. I felt like, as I grew older, moving became less like a part of my vocabulary. I felt like I had moved enough. But what could I say when God intervened in my life? I had to move again. And, indeed, we sadly had to move again. It was an agonizing journey.

Those things that did not fit in our new house I had to move to Diwang's house in Jonesboro. I liked our new home. I loved the space as well the privacy that my daughter and son-in-law gave us. It was convenient for us, because if I needed help, they were around and easily accessible. I also loved the idea that we could see the kids more often. All they had to do was come upstairs and bug us. There were times that Amy came to get her mom and would give me free time to be by myself. I loved to cook as long as I did not have to wash dishes. So they let me cook, and they cleaned up my mess.

At the very beginning, it was hard for Leth to adjust to our new home. She kept asking, "What are you doing to me, Mel? Why are we here? Let's go to our own home. When do we go home?" She once left the house and was very upset. I asked her to come back, but she didn't. I let her leave while I watched her from a distance, hoping that when she got tired she would come back. Well, she walked around the neighborhood, and then when it started to get hot, she went to the nearest house and tried to open the door. Fortunately, it was locked because the people probably went to work. I hurried to get her and then told her, "Honey, come on, let's go home." She thought the house she was opening was home. She could not understand how she got that far. All the things she was upset about earlier were completely forgotten, and she was happy again.

Meanwhile, I took the effort to find an Alzheimer's support group. The association in Iowa referred me to two contact groups in Athens. It was not hard to find one, and luckily enough it was also close to where we lived. It was a nice and friendly support group. I treasured this group because it helped me develop the strength to deal with my struggles with the disease. The church where Amy served was supportive too, especially when we joined two small groups: Sunday school and the Disciples study.

As soon as we were settled in the area, I started to develop my own routine. Wherever I went, Leth was with me. Even when I went to see my doctor, Leth had to come with me, unless Amy was not too busy to take care of her. It became an issue of safety and security for Leth when I had to do some business and had to leave her for a short moment. One time I went to the Veteran Administration Hospital in Augusta, Georgia, for my routine checkup, and I had to have some laboratory tests. Leth was with me, but I had to leave her in the lounge. I told her that under no circumstance was she allowed to leave the room. She agreed. But when I was done, she was gone. Fortunately, she did not use the elevator, so I found her wandering around that same floor looking for me. When she saw me, she was very upset and asked where I went.

I was concerned about what to do with her in the event that I needed to leave her and my kids could not help me. The Alzheimer's support group recommended several agencies that took care of elderly patients with dementia. A certified nurse or caregiver would come to our home, watch Leth, and be paid by the hour or day. It was very expensive, and the cheaper alternative was to take her to the day care center for the aging. I made arrangements to get Leth into the day care center. They asked me to come to their office with Leth so that she could start getting acquainted with the area before starting the program.

When I told Leth that she would be staying there more often, she got upset with me. She didn't like the idea. She warned me that she would never go to any day care center for the aging. She would rather be dead or lost. She said, "If you are getting tired of me, let me know and I will leave you now. Why don't you just divorce me or throw me out to the sea?"

I knew she was apprehensive, so I just listened and tried to give her peace of mind. I told her, "Your doctor highly recommended this for your healing. You need to socialize. You used to be a very social person prior to your sickness."

The words "healing" and "socialize" seemed to be effective, and amazingly she listened. She accepted the idea as long as I would be with her. I had to think about how to convince her that it was safe for her to be there without me. She would agree now, but I knew in a few minutes she would forget everything we talked about. But for whatever reason there were times she remembered everything we talked about. However, I was determined to take her to the Athens Adult Day Care Center. I was assured that those who worked there were trained to handle her since they dealt with patients like her all the time.

It was suggested that I needed to establish a routine and bring her there at least two or three times a week. I agreed. Perhaps it would be good for her to give it a try once a week and see how it went. The day finally came. I dressed her early in the morning, and she started asking me where we were going. I said, "Remember what we talked about? We will do what your doctor recommended and undergo social therapy." She said she remembered. Actually, I was not sure whether she really remembered or if she was just saying it because sometimes she didn't like to feel she was forgetful. So I went along with her mood willingly. The social therapy was important for her healing process.

As we entered the center, I sensed the resistance. She asked, "Why are we here, Mel? What are you doing to me?" I did not answer her back; instead I went directly to the nursing station. When Leth saw all those elderly patients, she turned around and told me, "I don't like it here. I am not that crazy. Why are you making me stay with these crazy old people?" She immediately turned around and went to the door. Fortunately, the door was closed and she didn't know how to open it. The nurses turned around, gently brought her back inside, and introduced themselves. As they talked to her, she was responding. They gave me the sign to leave without her noticing me. It was a big sigh of relief when I went out unnoticed.

I went back to pick her up around 4:30 PM. Our grandkids were with me, and Leth was happy to see us. The caregivers said, "Didn't we have a good time, Leth?" They mentioned everything they did, and Leth just nodded her head in agreement. Someone said, "Leth, be sure to come back again."

Leth amazingly agreed. "Yes, I will come back!" The nurse briefly reported that when I left, they kept her busy and just let her walk around and visit every room in the offices. She had no complaints. As patients started to get picked up by their family members, Leth started to get restless and asked for me all the time.

I felt good that night after that positive news. I was interested to know what she really did, but she couldn't remember anything. She said, "We did something but I don't remember." She was so tired that she went to sleep right after dinner. As usual, I did my nightly routine, stayed on my couch, and watched the evening news and a movie. Watching movies became my sleeping therapy. I watched and then went to sleep. So often I would watch the beginning of a movie and miss the rest, or I would catch it in the middle and then fall sleep again. Leth woke up because she needed to go to the bathroom. Once she found out I was not beside her, she started wandering around looking for me. She would wake me up, and then I would go to bed. This was our routine on most nights.

Since Leth loved to drive around, she and I would just drive around the city or neighboring areas, or sometimes we just went to Jonesboro to visit our son. We started an ambitious project to convert the old garage attached to our home in Jonesboro into a master bedroom. My son lived in our house. He rented the house so that I could pay my mortgage. He took in several tenants so that it would not be such a financial burden for him to pay the rent of this large house. I hired a carpenter to build us an extra room (the old garage) with a big bathroom that was handicap accessible. Furthermore, we wanted a kitchenette, a dining table, a small lounge.

The room was done in less than a month, and I knew it would be perfect indeed for Leth and me whenever we visited our son. We furnished it, bought a small refrigerator, a microwave oven, a toaster, kitchen utensils, two cabinets, a queen-size bed, and a leather sofa. It served as our own private room whenever we went to Jonesboro and a guest room when Diwang had company. I thought our first night would be great, but it ended up as a nightmare for Leth. She didn't understand what the room was all about.

She was upset that first night and told me that I was tormenting her by taking her to different places. She could not recognize that it was our home. But she listened to reason. However, after fifteen to thirty minutes, she would ask the same question and I had to explain it all over again. I confessed that I often just wanted to scream, but I knew that would not help her, so I just prayed for strength and patience. When I could no longer take it, I went out, got in my car, drove around the block, and screamed. It might be a crazy idea, but it helped me.

I finally realized that Leth could no longer tolerate moving to different places. On the other hand, what I built was not in vain. I added value to the house, and it would be my home whenever I went to Jonesboro. The room became a convenient place whenever I had guests or relatives staying overnight in Atlanta. They wouldn't bother Diwang or perhaps his wife-to-be. And indeed it became such an accommodating room when Diwang got married to Rebecca Davis. I felt good about the fact that in both places, Athens and Jonesboro, we had our very own room. It gave us a feeling of privacy, apart from our kids and in-laws.

Athens was now our home. We had a retirement place in the Philippines, too, that we would visit and stay for a while after Diwang's wedding, sometime in October 2008. We bought this place in preparation for our retirement. I had no idea that Leth and I would move sooner than we thought. However, Georgia seemed to be the perfect place for us, especially for me. The veterans hospital was not too bad for me to go to for a routine checkup. I liked their services and especially that the VA had a clinic in Athens. Leth's doctor was just around the block from our home. The neighboring area was peaceful, and it was a good location for walking.

We got to know more Filipinos in the city, and we joined their association. When guests came, we had a nice place to take them, like Stone Mountain, the botanical garden, the Coca-Cola headquarters, and CNN studio. We were not that far from Florida, the tourist spot of the world. Our favorite place was the home of the DAWGs, University of Georgia football stadium.

The city was not too big or too small. It was a university setting where you saw lots of college students, young people roaming around, and many foreign students. The city was full of early American history. I liked it because everything I needed for a simple life was there. My kids were around when I needed them. My grandkids were always with us, and we spoiled them with whatever we could afford.

Though I had not found the right hole yet to go fishing, I was sure I would find one sooner or later. The VA gave me a certificate so that I could secure a permanent license to fish and hunt in Georgia. I was also given a home free of property and vehicle registration taxes. God blessed me, not just financially, but spiritually. I was surrounded with love from my family and friends. What else did I need? God was good, and life was good indeed.

Every Sunday, Leth and I went to church and Sunday school. It was something we loved to do. On Wednesdays, we went to church also, and joined the community dinner, and attend Bible study. I also had some free time when I took Leth to the Athens Adult Day Care Center and when Amy took her mom around with the grandkids. On some weekends, we spent family time together with our daughter and her family, the Barkers. Diwang and Becca would also come to see us.

As Tre grew from a baby to a toddler, he developed some tricks that challenged his mom, dad, and grandparents. He discovered that Leth got irritated when she heard loud noise. When Tre would scream. She would stand up, cover her ears, and run toward our room, and bang the door. One time when we were quiet, Tre screamed, looked at Grandma, and watched to see what she would do. At times, Amy tried to stop him, but he wouldn't do it. He continued to challenge her. And with Ashtin, the challenge occurred mostly at the dining room table. I overheard Amy threatening to ground Ashtin if she did not eat her vegetables. Ashtin answered back, but it didn't matter. Since Ashtin loved to watch TV, Amy learned to use this for grounding her, and it worked.

But for Tre, grounding him would not work yet. Amy got irritated easily, but Rich had more patience in dealing with the two rascals. I loved watching them because it reminded me of Amy and Diwang when they were growing up. It was like watching history repeat itself. It was nice how Amy and Richard worked together to find ways to deal with their two active and healthy kids. I felt so blessed to have Amy and Richard and see how mature they were in dealing with their two kids. I hoped and prayed that their love for each other would remain truthful and they would become ideal role models for their kids, Ashtin and Tre, as they grew into adulthood.

Life was sometimes full of surprises. The good times were suddenly disrupted when I got the news that Leth was rushed to the hospital from the Athens Adult Day Care Center. I was told she had an accident. It was a moment that would change everything. Where God was leading us, I did not know. All I knew was that God was still with me, comforting me, helping me in my time of need.

Chapter 17

Life in Baler

Here we are, living in a big house with a licensed caregiver and a nurse who take care of Leth twenty-four hours a day. We also have a married couple who work as full time employees at the Beach House. The husband takes care of the security of our area and the building and area maintenance operations. The wife takes care of the kitchen, laundry, and housekeeping. We also have a manager who runs the total operation of our new home—or you might call it a private nursing home with only one patient, Leth. We call this place Ashtintin Beach House. The name Ashtintin was originally coined by my brother Carlos by putting together the names of the two great ladies of the Valdez and Puato families. Mel and Leth Valdez's only granddaughter is named Ashtin Barker, and Ramon and Uste Puato's only daughter is named Tintin Puato. Ashtintin Beach House will be converted into a retreat someday.

It has been almost three years since we moved into the Ashtintin Beach House (ABH). A lot of things have happened since then. We arrived in Baler and were welcomed with great hospitality. Bamba (Jonalyn Orpia) was introduced to us as Leth's licensed caregiver. Amelia is our housekeeper. Menyang was my mother's housekeeper who also came to join us since my mom (Ruth Alipio Valdez) decided to stay with us in this big house. Of course, Carlmax Frei Valdez, my nephew, was also with the group who seemed to be the general helpers and watchdogs of the operation.

Ramon and Uste Puato, who was my co-partner in this real estate endeavor, briefed us on what they had done in preparation for our coming. Now that I am here, I will take over and manage the entire operation. This couple lives in Plaridel, Bulacan, Philippines, and they come to Baler only when needed. Carlmax Frei, known as "Toknoy," was introduced to me by the Puato as the trusted person who was chosen to take care of the house. He is our nephew and is able to protect the interest of the house. Because I am new to the area and not acquainted with the way of living in Baler, I told Toknoy that I would make him my salaried manager to help me in the total operation of the house, including the hiring of all the helpers we need.

Toknoy is a college graduate, and so he deserves to be paid like any other professionals. At first, he said that he would be satisfied to stay with us and did not expect a salary, as long as he had food and a place to live. Prior to my coming to the Philippines, I had already made up my budget. I was determined to provide a competitive salary. But to my surprise, my calculations were higher than the actual salary I would be paying. On the other hand, I had neglected the fact that all these employees would need to be fed and I would have to pay for the utilities.

In spite of my miscalculations, I found out that I still had money left to take care of finishing the house. The first floor of the house was done well. I still have to finish the second and third floors. Per my and Toknoy's budget, we will be spending an average of $4,000 (or PHP190,000 a month based on PHP 47.50 per dollar exchange). Sometimes I had to use some of my contingency money to finance the big projects, such as putting in a concrete sidewalk from the beach to the river, creating living quarters for the helpers, buying generators in case of an electric outage, and buying a vehicle for our daily use. We also bought a boat in case there is a flood and the car can't pass. During the months of September to December, the waves were high and sometimes hit the highest level of the bank. They cut through and joined the river, which is less than a quarter of a mile away. When this happens, our property becomes an island. We have no way to leave except via boat to get to mainland Baler. The boat is also a great recreational vehicle for fishing and riding. We have a few more projects we need to finish to make our operation complete.

Bamba is a licensed caregiver. She took care of an elderly patient before joining us. The other caregiver is Levi Tingco, who took a two-year nursing course and also cared for an elderly patient. Bamba came first. I told Toknoy that Leth needed twenty-four–hour care. I needed one more caregiver, so we recruited Levi, who came after a week. These two seem to work well as a team. I have seen them doing well with Leth. They fed her by the beach even though the pathway was not cemented. They had to push the wheelchair hard because of the soft sand. Toknoy assisted them in going out and coming back to the house.

Sometimes I sneaked around and just watched what they were doing and how they were treating my wife. They sang songs to Leth, told her stories and jokes, read books to her, bathed her, and massaged her at night. (I hired a physical therapist to see Leth and teach our caregivers how to massage her.) The caregivers wrote a daily report of what Leth was doing and what they did to her. They knew I was reading it, and every fifteen days I gathered them and put them in my own file. Since they only had one patient, I expected that they would have lots of time to focus on and help Leth. I made it clear to all of our helpers that we were here in Baler for only one reason: Leth. Their job existed because of her, and therefore all must do their job well and take care of my wife.

I told them we were operating like a small nursing home except that we only had one patient, Leth. In addition to our caregivers, we have a manager who is responsible for all the operations of the house, and we have housekeepers responsible for the food, laundry, and cleanliness of the house and surroundings. We have a security and maintenance person responsible for the repairs and caring for the area. There was also a doctor who committed herself to come and see Leth when needed. Sometimes Dr. Myrna Nicer just came for an occasional visit.

After eleven months, Levi Sheila Tingco asked to be released so that she could continue her studies at nursing school. Brigette Sadaba was recruited. She was a nursing graduate from Wesleyan University, Philippines. Her presence, along with the doctor's, became a great asset to us. When Leth got sick, the doctor would give an order to our nurse, and then she would execute the order.

At one time she was ordered to inject Leth with dextrose, and she did. The nurse understood how to relate to the doctor when needed. She did not make just a daily report; she also documented what the doctor needed to know when something went wrong. Her knowledge and training helped me feel secure, because I knew that my wife was being monitored professionally. I was also pleased to see them in uniforms, even though they were in a house setting. I guess the manager required them to act and look professionally.

One weekend, Leth's two brothers, Caleb and Pongpong (Edwin), came to see her. It happened to be a day in October 2008 when Diwang and Becca were with us. This was the week after Diwang and Becca's wedding in Jonesboro. After the wedding they came to Baler to see their mother. The two brothers were invited to come so that they too would have a chance to see my son and his new bride. Leth was screaming then. She continued to lose her words, and when she tried to communicate, she sometimes screamed.

Leth's brothers saw their sister being taken care of very well. They all thought that her coming here was a good decision because of the quality attention and care she was receiving. The two brothers (Caleb and Edwin (aka: Pong Pong) thought that their sister still recognized them. They asked her, "Ate Bebe, do you know us?" So often she answered, "Yes!" My guess was that it was only a good guess. Leth did it to me too. When I asked her if she knew me, sometimes she would say yes, but other times she would say no.

So often she just guessed, and it was sometimes true but sometimes not. When my cousin came to see me, Leth was looking at both of us. My cousin, whom Leth had not seen since we got married, asked Leth, "Ate, do you still know me?" Her reply was definitely yes. Then he turned around and asked, "Ate, do you know this guy?" He was pointing at me. She said no. My cousin looked at me, laughed, and said, "I'm sorry, cousin. Ate doesn't know you."

Even the caregivers would ask Leth, "Tita, do you know me?" (*Tita* was a name that indicated familial closeness.) Again her answer was sometimes yes and sometimes no. My hunch was that she was guessing most of the time, and sometimes she just happened to get the right answer. However, even though she didn't know us, she seemed to feel secure, because she knew she was surrounded by familiar and caring people. She knew she was loved and taken care of.

Sometimes people who came to see her thought that she was not really sick and that she could recover in time if we just took her to those healers—for instance, a physical therapist named Edna, from Baguio, who came along with my cousin, or Dr. Anatalia Castrence, who had healed several patients who once could neither walk nor talk. According to Dr. Castrence, Edna was so good that she helped to relieved lots of Leth's pain. Her offer was irresistible. What could I say? I wanted my wife to get well, of course. The physical therapist was sure that she could make Leth stand, walk, and even speak again right after she saw her. Edna started right away with massage therapy, and she instructed the caregiver on how to do it in her absence.

Edna was very convincing, and she really made me believe. However, when Dr. Nicer came to visit Leth, I shared all my excitement with her. Dr. Nicer did not seem convinced, but she empathized and listened to me. Dr. Nicer told me that my wife's problem was neurological and that there was nothing wrong with her muscles. If Leth had a stroke, she could probably recover. But her problem was neurological. It was difficult for her to process the basics, such as standing, walking, talking, and feeding herself. This was not easy for a dementia patient. If Leth could only learn how to process all these actions in her mind, there was no doubt that she could get back into her normal activities. Her comments were not hopeful but perhaps more realistic.

Since Edna was persistent about helping Leth walk and talk again, I just went ahead and opened my house to her in case she was willing to come back. She promised us she would come back, and she did. She trained the two caregivers on how to do the massage to insure the continuity of the treatment during her absence. She went back to Baguio but promised to come back again to stay and complete the therapy for several months. She said that she needed to stay with us for at least three to six months to do the intensive therapy to make this work.

Since she would be staying for a while at our home in Aurora province, Edna first went back to Baguio said she would be back within the week. On the day that she was supposed to come, I waited for the call to pick her up at the bus station. There was no call. I started worrying because she did not make it as planned. I texted her and found out that she could not leave because she didn't have enough money for her travel fare. She asked for PHP5,000 in advance for her fare and some extra for the family she was leaving behind. I wired the money to Dr. Castrence, but I never heard from her again. I tried to text her, but to no avail. There was no response. Dr. Castrence told us that Edna took the money I wired and she had not seen Edna since. Meanwhile, we kept on waiting for her call and hoping that she would show up, but she never did. Her no-show was very disappointing to us, but perhaps it was also a blessing, because I was not sure that I could really trust her.

Edna had imparted some of her massaging techniques to the caregivers, which was helpful for them. Even though she was no longer around, Levy and Bamba used these techniques on Leth. Edna told them to massage Leth at one o'clock every morning. The rationale was that all of Leth's nerves were relaxed at this time, and the healing power of the massage would work more effectively past midnight. For several months, these two caregivers did what they were told. I watched them but never saw any improvement. The massage helped her to relax, and she seemed to enjoy it, but the healing power that Edna promised was not visible at all.

We also noticed Leth developing several behaviors that would come for a few weeks and then change again. At one time it was a pattern, and at other times there was no pattern. For instance, she developed a strange sound, like she was trying to clear her throat. She would say, "Khhhhhrrrrrrrrr." Instead of screaming, she would say this, as if she was very angry. So often she would be asked if she was upset, and she would say no and then sometimes laugh. Perhaps her most embarrassing behavior was when she started spitting. She spit all over and the caregivers had to put a bib around her neck, which she didn't like. I once tried to kiss her, which I usually did, and she spit in my face. So I said, "Why did you do that? You spit in my face." And she just laughed out loud.

When Leth created lots of noise, screamed, or spit, her caregivers tried to distract her with singing. Amazingly, Leth tried to sing along with them, and sometimes they would stop and Leth would continue and end the song. I was thrilled about this discovery, so I asked them to sing again while I tried to capture it on video. When she noticed I was taking her picture, she stopped singing. When she was restless, the caregivers would sing her favorite songs, and she would sing along. When she couldn't sing the lyrics, she would scream. Perhaps that was her way of expressing her anger and frustration. But the way she sang was so funny that we could not help but laugh, and soon enough she was laughing too.

There were times we found her sleeping—at least that was what we thought—but she would surprise us by suddenly laughing out loud. We found out that she was just listening to what we were talking about. She liked to hear funny words and jokes, and sometimes she just loved to hear people talking. At one time we were talking with some guests who came to see her. Perhaps she wanted to participate in the chatting, so she just screamed because she could only say a few words. Later the only words she said were "Hindi," "yes," "nor," and "Mer" (she used to say Mel). It was becoming more and more obvious that her vocabulary was limited. Sometimes someone would say "maban," and she would complete the word by saying "tot." *Mabantot* referred to the smell of poop or urine.

Her screaming could mean she was wet, she had a bowel movement, or she was hungry, thirsty, uneasy, in pain, or frustrated. Caregivers were alert enough to check all these symptoms, and it was easy for them to assess what she needed. It was hardest to find out when she was in pain or trying to say something that we did not understand. We would all get frustrated, but we needed to at least guess what she was feeling. Most of the time when everything was checked, the nonstop screaming had to mean that she was in pain. So we gave her pain relievers or sleeping pills, hoping that these would help to relax her. In most cases, it helped, but there were times that she had difficulty getting her sleep.

They usually fed Leth prior to our lunch and dinner. She would eat breakfast ahead of us only if she woke up early. When it was not raining, they would go outside with her while we were eating. She liked company, and she normally listened to what we were talking about while we were eating. Sometimes she laughed and we would look at each other, surprised that she was just listening to our conversations. She loved the company of familiar people, but she often got noisy when she heard many people talking at the same time. There were times I felt like she didn't like the company of unfamiliar people.

She did not move, except when the caregivers took her from the wheelchair to her bed and from the bed to her wheelchair. Since she didn't move a lot, she developed a habit of not moving her bowels for up to three days. We could tell quickly how irritable she was because she would scream nonstop. They fed her papaya and other food high in fiber, and that helped. But later even these foods no longer worked. Every morning they would take her to the bathroom, let her hang on the lifter, and wait until she had a bowel movement.

They tried to make a routine of going to the bathroom at nine or ten o'clock in the morning with the hope that she would develop a habit of releasing her stool every time they put her in the bathroom. There were times it worked, but then they had to use a suppository. But the suppository did not always help either. When this happened she would scream. I could not take her screaming, so I would just go where I could not hear her.

When I arrived in Baler, I slept beside Leth every night. But that changed quickly. The caregivers usually changed her in the middle of the night, sometimes once or twice or even three times. Her urination and bowel movements were more frequent in the first few months. Perhaps the adjustment and the constant moving we did from nursing home to home and then to Baler were the biggest factors in her inability to go to the bathroom. Since the caregivers were constantly changing her diaper and cleaning her at night on our bed, I made the decision to sleep on a single bed but still stay in the same room. That arrangement was favorable for me because I didn't have to wake up any longer during changing time.

Before going to sleep, I tried to go to Leth's bed and talk to her, tell her stories, and talk about our children and grandkids. Sometimes I went to her bed early in the morning when the caregivers were already awake and either cleaning the house or cooking breakfast. They were sensitive to me and encouraged me to spend more time with my wife. Sometimes I would send the caregivers to watch TV while I stayed with Leth on her bed. And sometimes I fall asleep in front of the TV, and they would wake me up and I would go to my bed.

The caregivers at first slept in another room with the other helpers. That arrangement was not helping me because when Leth started making noise, I had to go upstairs and ask them to tend to Leth. I decided that since our room was large enough for the four of us, I wanted them to consider staying with us in one room so that they were accessible to Leth. I had trouble going up and down the stairs, especially at midnight. When they heard my reason, nobody raised any questions. One caregiver had to stay with Leth in the bed, while the other stayed on the floor on a cushioned mat. I slept on a twin-size bed made of bamboo. It was directly across from Leth's full-size bed.

The arrangement worked well, because I didn't need to wake up anymore when they worked with Leth at midnight. Since the two caregivers went to sleep early to prepare themselves for the midnight work, I would sometimes go to the second floor and watch satellite television provider called Cignal to pass the time. Sometimes I let the caregiver watch TV first while I stayed with Leth and talked to her, told her stories about our past and our kids, or just gave her a hug, which she enjoyed. There were times when she responded as if she knew what I was talking about. Sometimes I saw tears in her eyes when I talked about our relationship and our kids. When I saw her responding that way, I too could not help control my tears.

When the caregivers were done watching television, usually at around 8:00 or 9:00 PM, they would come downstairs and get ready for bed. That was my time either to stay in bed and sleep or to watch television. So often I could not fall asleep easily, but once I started watching television I would snooze without even knowing it. It seemed like the television served as sleeping therapy for me. The caregivers would laugh because every time I watched TV, I would fall asleep. So when I woke up, either the TV was off (because someone turned it off for me) or a different program was on.

When Leth's US passport was about to expire, I had to find a way to renew it. She stayed for about a year in the Philippines. Since she was a US citizen, her extension had to be renewed too. I went to the US Embassy and applied for our US passports (because mine was about to expire as well). My passport was approved immediately, but Leth's application was not. The US Embassy required her physical presence. They told me to let her travel to the US Embassy because they wanted to see her in person. I had to explain that she was handicapped and bedridden. The interviewer still insisted that she needed to come unless we could get a court order in the province of Aurora.

Since I was no longer planning to take her back to the States due to her medical condition, I didn't see the significance of renewing her US passport. It was perhaps more practical for her to apply for dual citizenship so that she could stay as long as she needed. The dual citizenship was the easiest and most practical route I could take, and in less than a month it was approved. Now that she was both a Filipino and US citizen, I was saved the headache of renewing her visa as well as her US passport. Friends and relatives thought that was the most practical solution to Leth's looming deportation.

Since I came to the Philippines with Leth, I had been back to the United States twice. Every time I was separated from Leth, I really missed her. I felt so lonely, especially in bed at night. It was a strange feeling, because in the Philippines (where Leth and I were living temporarily) Leth had little to do with me. At times she didn't even know me. But every time I was away from her, I felt so alone. Perhaps just seeing her every day gave me the sense of security that I was with her.

At least I could say hi or talk to her. It always gave me great joy, even if she didn't know. But it gave me more joy when she responded to me with a smile or giggle. The caregivers bathed her each morning and I always greeted her with a kiss. It was comforting to know that she was being cared for and attended to 24/7. When I was away on a trip, I fantasized about making love to her again. However, once I got back from my long trip, my strong desire for her suddenly disappeared.

In my dreams, making love to her turned me on. It was so beautiful. I tried to ponder why my feelings would change suddenly. In my dreams she would respond, and I carried this fantasy home with me. But when I saw the reality, I didn't have the desire to make love to her. There was no chemistry or longing, which was really strange.

One night, I asked the caregivers if they would go watch television while I watched Leth. It was a great opportunity for them to get a break from Leth and also for me to get time with my wife. They obliged, and I was left alone with Leth. This time I hoped to recapture my feeling and my desire to make love to my wife. I tried to kiss her, put her arms around me, and hugged her tightly, but when I looked at her, she was looking at me unresponsively, perhaps wondering what in the world this man was doing. At that moment, I knew I was going nowhere, so I just stopped. I felt so stupid trying to force myself to make love to this woman who was no longer the woman I once knew. I felt like a stranger forcing myself on her, and she was a strange woman, or a child, or an innocent person who had no feelings or idea what was going on.

I was frustrated and ashamed. I started to thinking that it would be so gross if suddenly she urinated in her diaper or I found she had some stool and I had to clean it up before making love. Those thoughts did not help me at all in preparation to make love to her. Since I was turned off quickly by my thoughts of her, I closed my eyes, hugged and kissed her, and then told her stories about our past with our kids. She seemed to enjoy being hugged and kissed and listening to my stories. She knew how to listen, and once in a while she seemed to grasp what I was telling her and would laugh or smile. This little gesture gave me such satisfaction.

My feeling for her changed completely. It was like the feeling I had with my children when they were cuddly and fun to kiss and tell jokes and stories to. By doing so, I found complete satisfaction and joy every time I saw them. I had to face the reality and learn that I had already lost my wife, my playmate, my lover who gave me affection when I needed it. Though my wife's physical body was still alive, the Aleta I knew was gone. I felt like I had adopted a new member of my family, perhaps an adult with a child's mind, who could entertain me and make me happy whenever I was with her.

At times, I longed for a woman's touch, smell, affection, comfort, and love, especially when I was tired and lonely. I had to keep busy and try to prevent these thoughts from overtaking me. Seeing my wife being taken care of every day gave me a feeling of satisfaction. Also, seeing my projects being completed gave me a feeling of fulfillment. I felt like I was still worthy and could help people by giving them work, I could help young people go to school, and most of all I could go to church and help with their mission. Perhaps the greatest joy for me was looking forward to taking a trip to see my kids and grandkids every six months.

Sometimes I wondered if this would be my life at this stage. I had successfully raised kids, sent them to school, watched them get married, and witnessed them having their own children. (One is still waiting for the right time. When that will be, who knows?) Now the kids have their own lives away from their parents and are becoming independent. It is just Aleta and me now—as our covenant says, "in sickness and in health, to love and to cherish, 'till death do us part." I got sick, very sick at one time, and my wife took good care of me. Now she is sick, bedridden, and it is my turn to take care of her. Since her sickness is incurable, she deserves to be happy, taken care of, and live a quality life before she meets her maker. And I hope and pray that my covenant of faithfulness and love to God and my wife will remain.

I know that I am ready to let her go when the time comes and the good Lord takes her from us.

That readiness was tested when early one morning we heard her moaning. She was not loudly screaming, as she used to. She was moaning. Suddenly her nurse became panicky when Aleta started jerking and fainted in her arms. The nurse called me in a hurry and said, "Tito Mel, hurry! Tita Leth is gone!" The nurse was not sure whether to let her sit or lie down. She said, "Tita Leth, stay with me! Stay with me!"

I grabbed my wife, and she was no longer breathing. I laid her down and gave her mouth-to-mouth resuscitation. I pressed her chest and then gave her more resuscitation. Suddenly she coughed up some mucus and blood. After that, she started breathing again and was very quiet. I could not think of anything except taking her to the hospital quickly. I woke up CarlMax Frei (sometimes called Carl or Toks), my manager, and told him to call Leth's doctor and that we were going to take her to the nearest hospital.

Everything came quickly. Carl carried Leth to the front seat of the pickup truck while I drove. The nurse and Carl were holding Leth. We took her to the emergency room, and the medical staff responded well. The doctor decided to keep Leth for observation even though she seemed "normal" again. She started screaming when she did not like what was going on or the change of environment and the new people. The hospital staff sometimes didn't know how to handle her, and Leth's nurse helped them deal with Leth in taking her blood test, X-rays, etc.

That whole day, Leth was so noisy and screaming because of her discomfort with what was going on. The space was limited in her small hospital room. The nurse's hourly visit added more discomfort. Carl commented on Leth's unusual and nonstop noise all day. In the afternoon, Leth started to keep quiet and didn't respond to our jokes or even to the music. She sat quietly and stared at nothing. The second day, she was completely quiet and unresponsive. She was always sleeping, and if she woke up, she stared at nothing. This unusual behavior made me ask why this was happening to Leth. I was told that they sedated her and gave her lots of medication to control her aggression and shouting. The medication completely changed her behavior. She no longer giggled when she heard funny words, tapped her hands and feet with the rhythm of the music, or screamed when she was wet or hungry. These were all gone. She was always sleeping and just stayed quiet when awake.

I didn't like what they did to her, but it was too late because she was already loaded with all these repressive medication. The doctor told us that this could help her calm down, but when we got home we could start reducing the dosage until she got back to her normal pattern of behavior. Furthermore, the doctor reminded us that they found no serious problems from the lab tests and X-rays. The blood could be a gastric reaction to the pain medication she was taking. They gave her another medication to prevent this stomach bleeding. Since she had been diagnosed with dementia about twelve years ago, the doctor praised her length of life and attributed it to the quality care she was receiving.

I was warned that anything could happen because of her continued deterioration. The changes could be radical or mild. Instead of talking about her illness, her doctor diverted the discussion to a more positive one. She said, "We need to be thankful that Leth has reached twelve years, because Leth could be gone by now." Since there was no cure to this disease, we continued to give her tender loving care and hoped she would die without pain or suffering.

The hospital experience with Leth became another enlightening experience for me. I knew I could let her go without reviving her or giving her mouth-to-mouth resuscitation once she fainted or stopped breathing. I found that I was not quite ready when this happened. I could do nothing and let her die, but my instincts prompted me to save her life. I am not willing to let my love go. I know she asked me to let her go when this happened, and I agreed. But I've discovered that I am still not prepared to allow this to happen.

This will be a continuous challenge to my spiritual and emotional being. My mind is willing to let her go, but my spirit tells me to do the opposite, to save her. The next time this happens, all I can do is let God work in me. May my judgment be guided by my love of God and of Leth. May God give me the strength to make the decision when the moment comes!